SUFFOLK MYSTERIOUS MURDER

※

Mark Mower

To Lynda,

Best wishes,

M.a. Mower

COUNTRYSIDE BOOKS
NEWBURY, BERKSHIRE

C000140498

Cover designed by Peter Davies,
Nautilus Design

Produced through MRM Associates Ltd., Reading
Typeset by Mac Style, Nafferton, E. Yorkshire
Printed by Borcombe Printers plc, Romsey

Contents

Suffolk Lo

Eriswell ●

Mildenhall ●

● Great Livermere

● Fornham St Martin

Bury St Edmunds

Barrow ●   ● Horringer Mendlesham

Chevington ● ● Woolpit ●

Newmarket ●   Whepstead   Stowmarket

Stanningfield ●   ●

Hartest ●   ● Wattisha

Hundon ● Layenham ●

Glemsford ●

Kedington ●   Monks Eleigh

Long Melford ●

● Acton

Sudbury ●

Ballingdon   Ho

Boxford

n Map

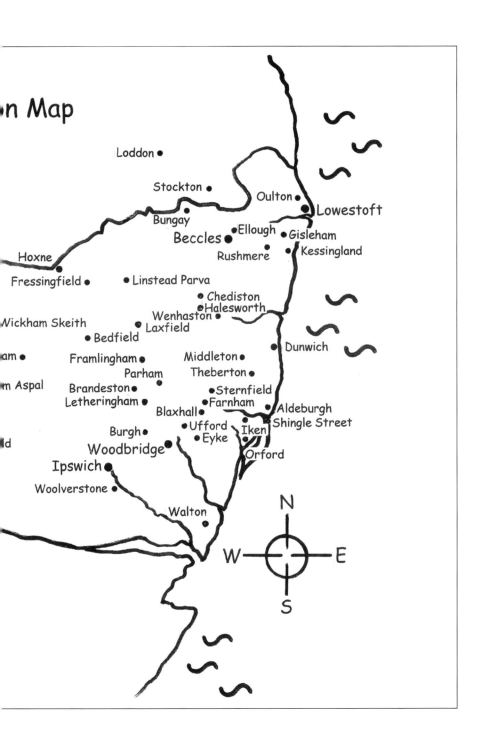

Loddon

Stockton

Oulton

Lowestoft

Bungay

Ellough · Gisleham

Beccles

Rushmere · Kessingland

Hoxne

Fressingfield · Linstead Parva

Chediston
Halesworth
Wickham Skeith Wenhaston
Laxfield

Bedfield

Dunwich

am · Framlingham Middleton

Parham Theberton

m Aspal Brandeston

Letheringham Sternfield

Blaxhall · Farnham

Aldeburgh

Burgh · Ufford Shingle Street

Iken
Eyke

Woodbridge

Orford

Ipswich

Woolverstone

Walton

N

W E

S

ld

INTRODUCTION

———❖———

Suffolk has a strong tradition of fabled yarns and fascinating folklore which contributes much to the rich diversity of its cultural heritage. From tales of husband poisoning and medieval slaughter, to urban ghosts and buried royal crowns, there is much to be enthusiastic about.

Alongside the accounts of murder from yesteryear, this collection contains stories about aquatic monsters, persecuted witches and four legged beasts. For good measure there are also chapters on mysterious stones and a wartime enigma on the Suffolk coast. Enough to keep even the most rational and reasoned of you wide-eyed and restless.

So get settled in a comfy chair and arm yourself with a mug or glass of your favourite tipple. It could be a long night.

Mark Mower

THE CASE OF THE ARSENIC DUMPLINGS

❖

One mile east of Long Melford, and close to the river Stour in the hundred of Babergh, is the picturesque village of Acton. As one of the largest villages in Suffolk it is home to a thriving rural community which benefits greatly from its close proximity to Sudbury and the market town of Bury St Edmunds. But it is also a village with a long and checkered history. Aside from the traditional ghost tales of supernatural hauntings by a coach and four horses, Acton was also the setting for one of the most infamous murder cases in 19th century Suffolk, and a crime that led to the public hanging of an 18-year-old woman in 1847.

The tale begins innocently enough. Catherine Morley had grown up in Acton and, like most of her contemporaries, had rarely travelled more than a few miles from her home. She lived with her mother, Maria Morley, and younger brother Thomas, in the middle cottage of a row of three thatched dwellings, close to the village church of All Saints. Their neighbours were a Mr Chinnery, a grandfather and local labourer, and a Mr and Mrs Simpson, who kept chickens on the meadow close to the cottages.

Like most children in the village, Catherine attended a local charity school and it was here that she first met her husband-to-be, John Foster. John was six years older than Catherine but had been sweet on her from the moment the two met. Maria Morley would later describe how John had pursued Catherine and expressed an early desire to marry the girl. And when Catherine left school at 14 to go into domestic service, the two had kept in contact. Catherine would write to John and he would occasionally visit her during the two years of her service in nearby Great Waldringfield and later at Bulmer in Essex.

By the time Catherine left domestic service in September 1846, the two youngsters were already courting. Catherine's mother later described their courtship as a happy one, although it seems likely that John's family was less keen on the match. When the two were married by Reverend Ottley at All Saints on Wednesday 28th October, John's mother and sisters were not present at the church and after the ceremony the pair were forced to live with Maria Morley, as they had done in the weeks leading up to their big day.

For his part, John worked on a local farm at Chilton for a Mr Meekings. Those that knew him would later portray John as a strong, healthy young man. This description was to prove highly significant in the light of what happened during the fateful days following the wedding. In that time John fell ill and died under extremely suspicious circumstances and the finger of blame was to fall squarely on his new wife of less than three weeks, the young Catherine Foster.

From the moment of their wedding, it does seem as if the marriage of John and Catherine had been hasty and ill-advised. Only three days after the ceremony, Catherine left home to stay with an aunt in Pakenham, not far from Bury St Edmunds. She said that she was keen to visit the aunt as she had had little opportunity to do so when in domestic service. John had apparently agreed for her to be away for up to a month, although Catherine promised to return earlier than this. There was a suggestion that John had pushed for them to wed before her departure when he had first learned of her plans. Neighbours would later claim that Catherine had said she should never have married John

All Saints' church in Acton, where John and Catherine Foster were married in Ootober 1846.

before the trip. The gossip in the village was that Catherine loved another man and had only married to please her mother.

We may never know whether the rot had first set in on the Foster marriage before, during or after the ceremony, but one thing is clear, John's death was a grisly and bizarre affair. Catherine returned home on Wednesday 11th November and a week later the farm labourer lay dead, poisoned it seems by her own fair hand.

It all began on Tuesday 17th November. John had gone to work as normal with workmate James Pleasance. Leaving work in the evening, the pair walked home together – John singing as they went. James left him at the gate of the Morley cottage in good spirits. Catherine herself had spent the day with John's mother, leaving at around five o'clock, and having earlier said that she must get home for John as it was 'dumpling night'. The quizzical mother-in-law had asked Catherine if she served up dumplings to her son every night. Catherine said not.

There must have been a large degree of determination and cool-headedness in the way that Catherine planned John's demise that day. In her subsequent trial, it was the testimony of her eight-year-old brother Thomas that proved most revealing. The young lad was pushed by the prosecution to describe how he had watched his sister preparing the supper that evening – a simple meal of dumplings, potatoes and tea. He testified how she had prepared the dumplings in a basin, how she had removed a paper bag from her pocket and poured a dark powder into the mixture and, finally, how she had burnt the bag, leaving no trace of the poison it contained.

Unaware of the fate awaiting him, John had entered the cottage to find a fire lit and Catherine and Thomas already tucking into their supper. His dutiful wife had risen to prepare his plate, taking a specially prepared dumpling from the copper cooking pot – a dumpling that was wrapped in its own cooking cloth.

John had no way of knowing that the meal served so carefully that evening contained heavy quantities of arsenic, a poison that would, over the course of the next 21 hours, burn the lining of his stomach wall with agonising and fatal results. His pain and decline began before he could even finish the meal. Overcome by nausea, and staggering out into the yard of the cottage, John was immediately sick.

Catherine followed her husband out of the cottage, retrieving what remained of the dumpling on his plate and re-wrapping it in its original cooking cloth. Testimony provided later by Mrs Simpson the next-door neighbour, suggested that Catherine then threw the food remains on the meadow outside the cottage. She found a piece of the dumpling and rather than waste the remains, crumbled the

The Morley cottage in Acton. (Foxearth and District Local History Society)

food before feeding it to her chickens (the hens subsequently died and when the crop of one of the birds was analysed it was found to contain traces of arsenic).

Maria Morley arrived home from her work as a washerwoman at around seven o'clock that evening. Ignorant of the crime that had been committed she found John already laid up in a room on the ground floor, seriously ill with bilious diarrhoea and vomiting up a dark liquid into a basin. He continued to be sick throughout the evening. The women went upstairs to bed before midnight, but were roused on several occasions throughout the night.

At eight o'clock the next morning, John was still alive but fading fast. Covering her tracks, Catherine walked the two miles to Long Melford to speak to Mr Jones, the local surgeon. Rather curiously she took a good two hours to get there and, when she did, her account of John's condition was later determined to have been misleading. She said that he merely had a bowel complaint, omitting that fact that he had been repeatedly violently sick. Jones suggested that it was probably a case of 'English cholera' (cases were apparently common the previous year) and gave her some powders containing mercury, chalk and rhubarb to remedy his condition. Catherine left the doctor saying that John had asked for him to call – something the doctor promised to do. She then returned home.

Maria Morley left the cottage at ten o'clock that morning and returned after lunch to find John in the last throes of death. By four o'clock the hapless husband had slipped away, watched over by the two women. John's mother, Elizabeth Foster, and his sister Susan, both arrived shortly after, stunned by the news and incredulous about his rapid demise. Elizabeth was keen to know whether John had asked for her before he died. Catherine confirmed that he had asked for both her and his sisters and brother, but said that she had been unable to leave him given his condition.

Unaware of the events that had taken place, Mr Jones the doctor arrived as promised at around five o'clock, surprised that the 'cholera' could have taken John so rapidly. However, he stuck by his original diagnosis and it was only after the coroner requested a post-mortem examination on the Saturday following the death that Mr Jones and another specialist carried out further tests.

The post mortem on 23rd November identified inflammation of the kidneys and an ulceration of the vena cava – a vein that returns blood to the heart – as the likely cause of death. However, Jones was careful to remove the stomach for further analysis – work that was carried out by Mr Image, a specialist in Bury. Image found large quantities of arsenic present and concluded that John had indeed been poisoned.

Catherine was promptly arrested and taken to Bury gaol. The police removed cloths and cooking ingredients from the cottage on 24th November. Tests revealed that one of the cooking cloths contained minute traces of arsenic, in spite of suggestions that it had been thoroughly boiled and washed. As a result, Catherine was indicted for the wilful murder of her husband. The trial was set to take place at the Suffolk Assizes.

In piecing together the case against her, the authorities were to rely heavily on the evidence provided by the young Thomas Morley. Catherine must have realised early on how damaging his testimony would be. On one occasion while she was in gaol awaiting trial, Catherine received a visit from her mother and Thomas. She berated Thomas with, 'You good for nothing little boy, why did you tell such stories?'

At the trial, the case for the prosecution was led by a Mr Gurdon. Catherine answered the charge of murder with a plea of 'not guilty'. Even at this stage the young bride seemed to have lost none of her earlier composure. On 27th March 1847, *The Bury and Norwich Post* described her performance by saying, 'The prisoner in the dock presented a most calm and collected demeanour. She was rather an interesting looking person…'

The prosecution maintained that the marriage of John and Catherine had not been a happy one and that in her comments before and after the murder, Catherine had demonstrated that she had little affection for her husband. There was also the damning testimony of her younger brother, which painted a vivid scene of cold, calculated homicide.

In her defence, Catherine claimed that John had complained of feeling poorly on the Monday night and John's sister in law did recall that John had mentioned having a slight headache on the Sunday. But this was not enough to convince the jury that foul play had not been involved. The rapid deterioration in the man's health only half an hour after eating his supper proved to be a crucial factor in implicating Catherine. Her concealment of the full nature of his symptoms to Mr Jones and the hard evidence of arsenic traces in the stomach, cloth and chickens merely sealed her fate.

The jury took only a quarter of an hour to find her guilty. Hearing the verdict, Catherine displayed no emotion and remained impassive. The Crown Court judge made the following statement in condemning her:

'Catherine Foster, you have been found guilty of the crime of murder ... it was your hand that put the poison in the food ... and ... it was wilfully done for the purpose of producing death of the individual you so lately married ... I may add that I entirely concur with the verdict, which the jury pronounced.'

He went on to say that the law required him to sentence her to death. A newspaper report on 29th March 1847 reported her reaction to this – 'The prisoner bore the sentence almost unmoved, merely applying a handkerchief to her eyes at the conclusion. We understand that she has since been more affected but not in a very great degree.'

While the trial was shocking enough to the local population, further revelations were to come. It appeared that the accusation of murder was not the first to be faced by one of the Morley family. Newspaper accounts only days after the conviction told of how Catherine's father, William Morley, had been suspected of robbery and murder during the inquest into the death of a William Kilpatrick in 1838. Kilpatrick had been found hanging by a rope from a direction post in Lavenham on the night of 18th July. The story was that Kilpatrick had collected his pension earlier in the day and had been with Morley. A witness had found Kilpatrick at around six-thirty that evening laying drunk in the road and claiming that he had been robbed of seven sovereigns. He said that if he had had a pistol he would have shot himself. The inquest concluded that suicide was the most likely cause

of death, although suspicion fell on William Morley. Guilty
or not, he was never charged with the murder.

Catherine Foster was the last woman to be publicly
executed in Suffolk. She was hanged in Bury St Edmunds on
Saturday 17th April 1847 before a crowd of 10,000 on
Market Hill. Prior to the execution, she was visited by
Reverend Ottley of Acton, who had conducted her marriage
ceremony only six months earlier. At his suggestion she sent
the bible he had given her at the wedding to her husband's
mother. History has not recorded how Elizabeth Foster
received this memento.

An anecdotal account given of the hanging some years
later, provided a vivid recreation of the scene – 'The poor
woman … gave a heart rending speech from the scaffold
imploring other young women, who may be tempted as she
was, not to follow her example, but to stand firm and stick
to their marriage vows.'

It was an event that shocked many, including the Marquis
of Westmeath, who raised the issue in the House of Lords
later that month, calling the attention of the Government to
the conduct of the execution and the disgust of the
spectators. And while there appeared to be little doubt about
Catherine's guilt, it was equally clear that many felt
uncomfortable with the continued use of capital punishment
in such cases. The first attempt at reform had occurred only
seven years before, in March 1840, when 90 Members of
Parliament voted with the abolitionist William Ewart to do
away with the death penalty altogether. Despite this, and the
growing public disgust with executions, it would take over
100 years for capital punishment to be finally abolished.

After the execution Catherine's body was taken to Bury
gaol where a cast was made of her head for phrenological
reasons. On her body was found a badly written letter
addressed to her mother. It read simply and somewhat
naïvely, 'Dear Mother, I have no wish to live, I hope you will
make yourself happy about me, I have great hopes of going
to heaven.'

THE WAVENEY RIVER MONSTER

❁

Stories about unusual sea serpents and river monsters can be found in almost all parts of the United Kingdom. From the infamous Loch Ness Monster in Scotland to the humpbacked 'Morgawr' in Falmouth, there are numerous tales about aquatic creatures that have challenged biologists and defied public belief. And Suffolk too has its fair share of yarns about the beasts that lurk beneath our waves and waterways.

Alongside the oft-quoted tales of a Nessie-like creature known as the 'Kessingland Sea Serpent', there have also been rumours of a mysterious, water-borne, creature in the inland waterways of east Suffolk. The most notable sighting of the so-called 'Waveney River Monster' occurred in the 1980s, when two coypu catchers saw the unusual animal while on patrol in a small boat. The creature itself was every bit as strange and elusive as the coypu they were paid to hunt down.

The two Beccles men were employed full-time by the then Ministry of Agriculture, Food and Fisheries (MAFF) to track, catch and exterminate coypu. These large semi-aquatic rodents are native to South America and were first introduced to the British Isles in 1929 when fur farms were set up in Sussex, Hampshire, Devon and Norfolk. The farms were established in lowland areas, rich in rivers and streams. When a number of coypus escaped from fur farms in the 1930s, they were quick to breed and proved highly successful in evading capture and thriving in the East Anglian countryside. Growing to around a metre in length, the large rodents eventually bred to such an extent and consumed such vast amounts of sugar beet that a dedicated 'Coypu Control' unit was set up to eradicate them. This was finally wound up in the late 1980s and there have been no confirmed reports of coypu in the wild since December 1989.

Colin Denny and Noel Rochford saw the river creature on 19th March 1984, on a bright and clear Monday morning. They were in a small boat patrolling the waters between the Waveney Inn at Burgh St Peter and Somerleyton, checking their traps and watching out for coypu. They spotted what looked like a log in the water, some 15 yards from them, only to realise that it was a living animal, very much bigger than any coypu. For the next 20 minutes or so the two men caught over a dozen glimpses of the creature as it moved above and below the surface, travelling comfortably through the water and moving at speed when it needed to.

'I have never seen anything like it in my life before', said Mr Denny, when it was reported in the *Beccles and Bungay Journal* later that week. 'It probably weighed about 300 to 400 pounds. It was a very unusual creature.' He described it as having a large head like a moose, with large nostrils and big eyes. Its broad back was about two feet wide and it had coarse rust brown fur. His colleague, Mr Rochford, claimed to have seen the beast three or four times prior to this. He described it as 'big, powerful and gruesome-looking'.

The two men admitted to being 'inquisitive and apprehensive', but even though they were armed with standard .22 calibre pistols as part of their role, they had no intention of killing or harming the animal. Mr Rochford added that, 'We didn't try to overtake it and we didn't try to get too close. It seemed to be looking at us, rather than us looking at it.'

In the aftermath of the sighting, a local holiday company offered a £10,000 reward for proof of the river creature's

Colin Denny and Noel Rochford – two coypu catchers who saw a 'river monster'. (Beccles and Bungay Journal)

existence, but only if the observer was using one of their boats and the creature was not trapped or harmed. No one came forward to claim the prize.

The press coverage also led to much media speculation about the type of animal the men had seen. Checks with the local Otter Trust at Earsham confirmed that it was unlikely to be an escaped muntjak deer. A local naturalist suggested that it could be a bull Atlantic grey seal that had come up the river from the coast. Norwich zoologist and geologist Philip Cambridge believed the animal might be an escaped capybara, the world's largest rodent and, like the coypu, a native of South America. Co-incidentally, the capybara is the only rodent mammal larger than the coypu.

Retelling the story years later, Colin Denny believes that the water-borne animal may well have been a capybara. Having family in the United States, he has seen wild moose close up and is convinced that what he saw that day in 1984 was most likely to have been the giant, guinea pig-like creature, suggested by Mr Cambridge. The zoologist said at the time that such a creature would float, 'with only its eyes and nose above the water, and there is a fair chance you would not see it. It might seem to disappear, but it's just floating'.

Weighing in at anything from 80 to 145 pounds, an adult capybara is distinguished by its two, sharp-edged, incisors

The Capybara grows to about 3ft in length. (www.copyright-free-pictures.org.uk)

and can vary in colour from brown to red and all the colours in between. Its skin is tough and thinly haired. The name 'capybara' means 'master of the grasses' in the language of the Guarani Indians. While clumsy on land, the rodent is an excellent swimmer and can dive and stay under water for several minutes. It can even sleep underwater, with its nose sticking out of the water. As such, the men's description of the river monster does seem to have similarities with the world's largest rodent – although it does not begin to explain how one may have ended up swimming freely in the waterways of east Suffolk.

Whatever the two coypu catchers saw that day remains a mystery. Like the sightings of the Kessingland Sea Serpent, its appearance remains both intriguing and tantalising. A rare glimpse, perhaps, of a singularly unique and elusive Suffolk monster.

THE SHOOTING OF
P.C. MCFADDEN

———————❁———————

It was William Schwenck Gilbert who first penned the memorable line, 'A policeman's lot is not a happy one', in the 1879 opera, 'The Pirates of Penzance'. It seems an apt description of the general state of policing in Suffolk during the Victorian period and a particularly suitable elegy for one unfortunate officer, Police Constable James McFadden. He remains one of only a handful of officers to be killed while on duty in the county.

For many centuries, policing in Suffolk relied on a rudimentary system of parish constables – a system not out of keeping with the small, isolated, rural communities that defined the county until the 1830s. But with sweeping industrialisation, significant population growth and the widespread migration of workers away from the countryside, it was recognised that the police service itself needed to modernise and become a more professional organisation. One that was better able to deal with some of the social unrest caused by technological transformation and changing economic conditions.

The 1830s and 1840s saw the first attempts to establish a professional policing structure in Suffolk, centred on a number of individual force areas. These covered the east and west of the county, Ipswich, Bury St Edmunds, Sudbury, Beccles and Southwold. But the new arrangements would take time to bed down and officer discipline, in particular, would remain a consistent problem throughout the Victorian era.

It was at this time that James McFadden was sworn in as a new police constable in the Kessingland area. Working conditions at that time were not easy. Hours were long and there were no recognised breaks. McFadden was required to wear his uniform at all times outside of his home and could be docked pay for minor irregularities like poor spelling. He could not even marry without the permission of his superiors. Among the rules of his appointment were the requirements to act with 'moderation and humanity' and to perform the role 'without malice and partiality'. He was expected to keep the peace, capture those committing crime, and transfer them up to the quarter sessions or whatever court was sitting for trial.

On Thursday 27th July 1844, P.C. McFadden was given the job of guarding some farm buildings in Gisleham owned by a Mary Button. This would not have been an atypical job for a constable at that time and petty theft from agricultural premises was a frequent enough misdemeanour. But the shooting of the officer in a barn close to the Button's home, on the evening of Sunday 30th July, was anything but commonplace.

There can be little doubt that William Howell (28), his brother Walter (21) and colleague Israel Shipley (38) had planned to rob the Button's barn that evening. Shipley later confessed as much to a fellow inmate at Beccles gaol. But it is unclear whether any of the men planned to kill, even allowing for the fact that the older of the Howell brothers was known to have had an earlier run-in with the hapless officer.

A witness at the eventual trial of the three men testified that some three weeks before the shooting she had been travelling by cart from Beccles to Hulver on a turnpike road when she saw P.C. McFadden. William Howell was in a pony cart coming in the opposite direction and had passed by very close to the police officer. Harriet Botwright heard McFadden cry out, 'Mind old feller how you drive!' She then heard Howell reply, 'Damn my heart if I should not like to drive over you.' On hearing this McFadden threatened to take the matter further, but Howell continued to throw insults at him. The witness thought Howell had been drunk at the time.

On the evening of the shooting, it was Harriet Botwright herself who tipped McFadden off that trouble was in the offing. On leaving her Hulver home at around eight o'clock, she travelled across the marshes, passing William Howell's cottage. She claimed to have seen Israel Shipley not far from his own home, with William Howell close by in a small enclosure. Walter Howell had apparently passed by a few minutes later. All appeared to be heading in the direction of Mutford Hall. Botwright knew all three men to be petty criminals. She said she later spied them, with others she recognised, some one and a half miles from Mrs Button's farm.

Meeting up with McFadden in the Button's garden, Botwright raised the alarm and spoke to the police officer for a short while before the thieves arrived. She later claimed to have seen five men, but could only swear positively to the identification of the Howell brothers. William Howell was described as wearing a black velvet frock coat and a hat. She left the farm at this point fearing danger.

The precise nature of what happened next remains unclear. But, based on the evidence presented at the trial, it would appear that P.C. McFadden had watched William Howell unlock and enter the barn door, followed closely by his brother Walter and Israel Shipley. He had then pursued them into the barn. The thieves told McFadden to go back but he refused. There was a continuing exchange of words and at some point William Howell discharged a shotgun at McFadden. Walter Howell and Shipley then walked over to kick the wounded police officer.

Harriet Botwright testified that she heard the gunshot about half an hour after she had left the farm. Returning briefly to the crime scene she saw McFadden lying outside the back door of the Button's home, groaning in pain. Fearing that the robbers might then attack her, she headed off.

Mary Button opened the door to McFadden and found him wounded and in agony. She got him into the house, but could do little to tend his wounds and recognised that he needed a doctor. The police officer told Mary that he knew who had shot him.

In the early hours of Monday morning P.C. McFadden was taken by farm cart to the police station in Kessingland. Here he was seen by John Prentice, a Lowestoft surgeon. Prentice climbed onto the wheel of the tumbrel and asked, 'Mac, how are you?' McFadden replied, 'Oh Doctor, I'll never get over this.' The doctor then had him moved to a bed and ordered some brandy and water be dispensed. He later described the wounded police officer as being in severe shock and heavily soaked in sweat.

Prentice undressed McFadden and examined his injuries. He found an extensive gunshot wound in the front of the officer's left thigh. There was one hole larger than the rest, about an inch and a half in depth, caused by a substantial grouping of shot. And while there were several other perforations, these were not felt to be significant.

A senior officer was called for. Superintendent Lark arrived and had a conversation with McFadden around five o'clock in the morning. He asked if the constable knew who had shot him. McFadden replied, 'Yes, Howell.' Lark then asked where the offender lived and the officer said, 'Hulver'. When asked to describe what William Howell was wearing, McFadden said the man wore a hat and a long velvet coat down to his knees. Asked if he would recognise the robber again if he saw him, McFadden confirmed, 'Yes'.

For P.C. McFadden this was to be a cruel and untimely end to his policing career and his life. He finally passed away on Tuesday 1st August 1844. On the basis of his evidence, the police arrested the Howell brothers and Israel Shipley and charges were brought against them.

The trial took place at the Suffolk Assizes on 10th December 1844. The prosecutors in the case were a Mr Gurdon – the same man who had successfully prosecuted Catherine Foster, the Acton poisoner (see chapter 1) – and a Mr O'Malley. Defending the three men was a Mr Prendergast.

Alongside the testimony from Harriet Botwright, Mary Button, surgeon John Prentice and Superintendent Lark, the prosecution called James Plum to the stand. He was a prisoner being held in Beccles gaol at the same time as Israel Shipley. He described how he had been walking in the misdemeanour yard of the gaol one day and had asked Shipley what he was in for. Shipley said it concerned the shooting of a policeman. Plum then asked whether Shipley's partner had shot the police officer, to which Shipley replied, 'Yes'.

When asked about names, Shipley said his partner in crime was William Howell, together with William's brother Walter.

At the end of the trial Mr Justice Williams summed up the evidence. The jury then retired, taking only ten minutes to return with a verdict of guilty against all three prisoners. Williams then addressed the prisoners and announced that each would face the penalty of death by hanging.

The prisoners listened to the verdict without any apparent emotion. At the end, Walter Howell addressed the judge by saying, 'Do you reckon, my Lord, you have done your duty? Every witness I have had up against me I can prove liars!'

Throughout the trial, it appears that Harriet Botwright's testimony was central to the case against the men. And yet her own, seemingly cowardly, conduct went unnoticed. It is strange, that having recognised the men to be up to no good and having forewarned P.C. McFadden, Botwright should make no effort to summon further help. Even when she found the police officer to be severely wounded, she appeared to think only of her own safety and left without assisting or raising the alarm. Her errant behaviour certainly warranted more attention than it appears to have been given at the trial or in the publicity that followed.

In spite of the sentence of the court, there was to be a last minute reprieve for Israel Shipley and Walter Howell. A respite from execution was received from the Secretary of State on 24th January 1845, commuting their sentence to one of transportation. In due course, both men were transported to New South Wales in Australia to serve out their years.

For William Howell, as the undisputed ringleader of the gang, the outcome was to be very different. In the lead up to his execution, Howell was visibly emotional but stalwartly refused to admit any guilt in the murder of P.C. McFadden. At one point he was heard to say, 'If my brother Walter is reprieved, I should not mind dying.'

At midday on 25th January 1845, he was led by a chaplain up to the gallows outside the County Courts in Ipswich, hooded and with his hands tied in front of him. When prayers had been read he asked to have the hood removed from his head and before the large crowd of onlookers announced, 'My dear friends, here I stand – but I die innocent.' William Calcraft, one of the best known of all executioners at that time, then adjusted the rope around Howell's neck, before making his way down from the execution platform and positioning himself close to the cord which supported the drop, with a drawn knife. When the chaplain had commended the prisoner's soul to God and dropped a handkerchief as the recognised signal, Calcraft severed the cord to complete the hanging and the despatch of William Howell.

P.C. James McFadden was not the only police officer killed in action during the 19th century, but his tale lives on as a shocking and tragic reminder of the perils faced by the

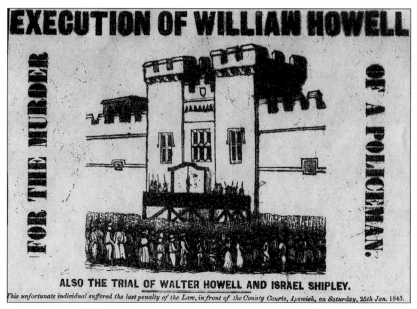

The execution poster for the hanging of Walter Howell on 25th January 1845. (Suffolk Record Office)

many men and women since that time who have served in the war against armed and dangerous criminals. It is to them that we owe a continuing debt of gratitude.

WITCH HUNTS AND WITCH TRIALS

─────────── ❁ ───────────

Like other parts of East Anglia, Suffolk has a long history and tradition of paganism, folk magic and herbalism. It has also been the scene of a remarkable number of witch hunts and witch trials throughout the centuries, many of them undoubtedly resulting from official misunderstanding and hysteria about these alternative beliefs and country practices. In effect, a significant number of innocent people suffered as a result of this religious bigotry and spiritual zeal.

Even before witch hunting began in earnest, Suffolk had its fair share of religious persecution. John Noyes, a shoemaker from Laxfield, was sentenced to death for his religious beliefs in 1557. He was burnt at the stake on 21st September, his last words being, 'Lord, have mercy on me! Christ, have mercy upon me!'

The Catholic Church first declared its official opposition to witchcraft in 1484, with a papal bull allowing for the 'correcting, imprisoning, punishing and chastising' of those guilty of 'incantations, charms and conjurings' and 'other abominable superstitions'. However, it was not until 1563, with the collapse of Roman Catholicism in England, that the death penalty was prescribed for the first offence of anyone found guilty of using witchcraft. Witch hunting in East Anglia began soon after this with the first major witch trial taking place in Chelmsford in 1566.

The legal process of pursuing 'witches' appeared to be heavily centred on the Biblical dictum, 'thou shalt not suffer a

Early woodcut print of a witch, c. 1643.

witch to live' which gave the practice some kind of moral standing. Subsequently, scapegoats were sought. Anyone deemed to be unusual or out of step with the established community could be singled out for persecution. As a result, cases were brought against a wide range of people, including midwives, folk magicians, assertive women, eccentrics and disabled people. Even something as straightforward as a birthmark could be construed as evidence of 'the devil's mark'.

Most alleged witches were poor, older women. Many underwent torture using barbaric practices like 'pilnie-winks' (thumb screws) and metal 'caspie-claws' (heated leg irons) to extract a 'confession'. It was little wonder that so many confessions contained strange and unbelievable claims of supernatural practice. It was only by confessing that victims were spared further torment.

The most bizarre test of a witch's guilt was the practice of 'swimming' or ducking in water. The theory was that water repelled servants of the devil – if a witch or wizard floated or failed to sink in water it was a sure sign of their guilt. Originally used as a general test for all crimes under English law, it became a popular, if unofficial, test for witchcraft for over five hundred years.

There was no shortage of people willing to point the finger at alleged witches. As early as 1562, a Cambridgeshire doctor, William Bullein, published a book against the practice of witchcraft in which he wrote, 'I did know within these few years a false witch called Mother Line, in a town in Suffolk called Parham, which with a pair of ebony beads and certain charms, had no small resort of foolish women when their children were sick. To this lame witch they resorted to have the Fairy charmed and the Sprite conjured away.'

The established Church began to take action against many traditional Pagan folk practices like divination, curses, spells and magical healing, declaring them all to be evidence of witchcraft. And from 1604, with the backing of the Protestant King James I, witch hunting was given added impetus when any attempt to cure illness by unauthorised means was declared to be witchcraft and therefore punishable by death.

A second wave of witch hunting began in earnest in 1644 after the English Civil War, under the direction of Matthew Hopkins, the self-proclaimed 'Witch-Finder General'. Hopkins' reign of terror lasted until 1647 when he died of tuberculosis. By then, some 300 people had been tried and executed, and many were in East Anglia.

Hopkins of course had a vested interest in pursuing all alleged offenders. He was paid a fee for every 'witch' he prosecuted. A number of Suffolk towns willingly paid him to help rid them of witches – Aldeburgh paid him £6 and Stowmarket £23, at a time when the average daily wage was 6d (or 2.5p).

The campaign had devastating results across Suffolk. In 1644, 40 people were hanged for witchcraft near Bury St Edmunds. A woman known as 'Mother Lakeland' was burnt

Woodcut print depicting Matthew Hopkins.

at the stake in Ipswich during September 1645 for, supposedly, bewitching her husband to death. Mary Lakeland was alleged to have been a 'Professor of Religion' for many years and under the direction of the devil – the tools of her trade being three imps, two little dogs and a mole. She confessed to her crimes after being swum.

Across the county, war was waged on anyone thought to be in league with the devil. In trials mirroring the infamous Salem witch hunts in America, people were rounded up and faced their accusers for all sorts of tenuous reasons – it could be a very effective way of getting rid of annoying neighbours! Ten people from Halesworth were tried for witchcraft and four were hanged at Bury. In Stowmarket, Hopkins tried seven people; Richard Foreman, Good Mills, William Keeble, Margaret Powell, Goody Low, Mary Fuller and Elisabeth Hubbard. After being tortured, Faith Mills of Fressingfield, confessed that her pet birds had forced a cow to jump over a stile. She too was hanged for witchcraft.

A large number of witch trials were held at Framlingham at this time, the modern day duck pond close to Framlingham Castle being known then, more infamously, as the 'Ducking Pond'.

It was not just old, misunderstood or disabled people that suffered. With no legal counter-argument against a charge of witchcraft, cases were brought for other religious or political purposes. At Brandeston, John Lowes, a Christian minister and Royalist sympathiser during the Civil War, was singled out for treatment. After being kept awake for days and swum at Framlingham to produce the desired result, Lowes confessed to sinking a ship off Harwich using black magic. In spite of the absurdity of the 'confession' and the fact that no ship was known to have sunk, he was found guilty and hanged at Bury St Edmunds.

It seemed that some old scores were being settled under the guise of religious zeal. Other 'scandalous ministers' were tried at Theberton and Ufford after their activities on the

Sabbath had been examined and evidence of their wayward rituals had been assembled.

After Hopkins, witch hunting continued sporadically throughout Suffolk. And while it tended to be less well organised, this did not prevent a number of high profile cases from coming to court, the most notorious of which was the trial of Amy Duny and Rose Cullender in March 1665.

The women were widows and lived in Lowestoft. Rose was the younger of the two and the niece of Amy. They lived close to each other and both were neighbours to Dorothy Durent, on whose evidence the women were first indicted for supposedly bewitching local children.

Their trial took place at the Bury Assizes. Three of the children who had allegedly been bewitched were brought to the courthouse to give evidence. But on entering the main hall of the proceedings, all three appeared to fall into strange and violent fits, before apparently being struck dumb. For the remainder of the trial they were unable, or perhaps unwilling, to give any useful evidence.

The case against Amy centred on her supposed mistreatment of Dorothy Durent's infant child, William. Leaving her home earlier that year, she had asked Amy to look after William in her absence and had agreed to pay her a penny for doing so. She had specifically requested that Amy did not suckle the child while she was away. When she returned, she was angry to learn that her wishes had been ignored and Amy had indeed suckled the baby. In the argument that ensued, Amy reacted aggressively towards Dorothy, taking the moral high ground and threatening the mother.

Dorothy went on to claim that later that night, William had fallen into a strange fit and was overcome with melancholy for several weeks afterwards. Concerned at the baby's condition, she had sought advice from a Dr Jacob in Great Yarmouth who had a reputation for helping children who had been 'bewitched'. He advised the concerned mother to hang the child's blanket in the corner of the chimney during the day. When wrapping the baby in the blanket at night, the doctor further suggested that if she found anything untoward, she was not to be afraid and was to throw whatever she found onto the fire.

In her testimony, Dorothy said that she had followed the doctor's advice and one evening when she came to put the baby to bed, had discovered a large toad in the blanket. She called for one of her other sons to catch the creature and when it was held over the fire with some tongs, the toad had made a terrible noise before exploding like the discharge of a gun, upon which it apparently disappeared.

The court then heard that Rose Cullender had visited Dorothy and told her that Amy was in an awful condition, her face having been scorched with fire. Indeed, when Dorothy then went to see Amy, she found the woman's face, legs and thighs were all covered in burns. When asked what had caused the injuries, Amy had apparently blamed Dorothy.

In the course of the proceedings, other evidence was heard, suggesting that both Amy and Rose had been practicing witchcraft. To the charges brought against them, both women pleaded 'not guilty' and, refusing therefore to confess, the two were duly sentenced to death by hanging – the case itself demonstrating just how absurd and inadequate the English justice system was at dealing with cases of this type.

The last official execution of a witch in England occurred in 1722, although it would be wrong to imagine that witch hunts ceased at that point. In Suffolk, as elsewhere, local communities took it upon themselves to pursue people who they believed were responsible for sickness, death and disease and any unusual adversity experienced in the countryside.

Witches were often held to be responsible for everything from the blight on corn to adverse weather conditions and scapegoats were sought accordingly. In September 1752 the *Norwich Gazette* reported that villagers in Stonham Aspal had tied up two or three old people with sheets and cords before swimming them in the belief that they were responsible for poor harvests and the loss of some cattle.

Others were singled out for equally absurd reasons. In December 1748 Alice Green of Monk's Eleigh was accused of being a witch after she attended church wearing a black silk dress. Countering the charge, she volunteered to be swum in order to prove her innocence. In July 1776 a man at Farnham accused of being a wizard was swum in the River Deben, watched by a large number of spectators from across the county. His hands and feet were tied and the man only survived because of the intervention of a concerned bystander. A similar case occurred in 1792 when a supposed witch was discovered in Stanningfield and was swum by onlookers in a village pond close to the church.

Isolated cases of witch punishment continued well into the 19th century. In July 1825 at Wickham Skeith, local people attacked Isaac Stebbings, an itinerant beggar, for allegedly bewitching a cobbler's trade. Tying his hands they threw him into a pond three times before the local vicar and churchwarden intervened and the unfortunate wretch escaped the clutches of the mob.

Other incidents confirmed that hysteria about witchcraft continued to be a feature of rural life. In February 1829 *The Bury and Norwich Post* reported a case at Ballingdon, near Sudbury, where three women took it upon themselves to tackle a neighbouring labourer who was believed to be 'in bad handling'. The women cut off his finger and toe nails and some of his hair before putting them in a glass bottle and placing this on a fire to ward off evil spirits.

Numerous other accounts testify to the existence of wise women and supposed witches throughout Suffolk. The obituary of Frances Harris from Chevington on 27th September 1859 described her as, 'a very aged woman who for many years imposed on the credulous by her reputed witchcraft until the magic implements containing her "spells" was destroyed by the request of Lord Arthur Harvey and Lord Alfred Harvey'. Similarly, the Reverend Hugh Pigot, writing in 1863, said, 'I met in a cottage in Hadleigh a woman from Whatfield who proved to be a devout believer in witchcraft.'

In her book, *Witchcraft in England*, Christina Hole provides an account of an alleged case of witchcraft as late as 1890. An inquest was held in April of that year following the sudden death of a baby girl in Fressingfield. The medical evidence suggested that the death was due to shock caused by the external use of a powerful irritant. The parents said that the infant had been in the care of a Mrs Corbyn, who had died on the same day. They claimed that she had told them on her deathbed that the baby would not survive for very long after her. Later when they removed the child from its pram, they were stunned to see smoke rising from it. When they reached home the baby had died. Mrs Corbyn's husband, George, told the jury that he had always believed his wife to be a witch and had taken all steps to avoid upsetting her.

The isolated and insular nature of some parts of the county does help to explain how the hatred of witchcraft and hysteria about its effects gathered pace during some of Suffolk's darker periods of history. But at a time when the immigration and asylum debate continues to fill headlines and religious intolerance is again under the spotlight, it does seem as if witch-hunting and scape-goating of a slightly different nature continue to be features of our modern lives.

OF THE FATHER AND THE SON

❖

By its nature, parricide, or parent killing, is a rare and startling phenomenon. Despatching those who have given you the very breath of life seems both cruel and ironic. No wonder then that legal systems the world over have sought to single out this crime as being one of the most pernicious of human acts. In ancient Rome, those found guilty of parricide were sewn into a sack, along with a dog, a cockerel, a snake and an ape, before being cast into the sea – a singularly insidious punishment. In 18th century Suffolk, the crime met with a more traditional penalty – the taut end of a hangman's noose. It was a fate that was to befall 25-year-old Charles Drew.

Charles Drew senior was a successful attorney who had acquired a considerable estate and resided in a large house in the town of Long Melford. Alongside his main property, he also owned a smaller house on the main street of the town which he used as his office and which he lodged at from time to time. It was here on the night of 31st January 1740 that the retired lawyer was shot and murdered at close range and in cold blood.

The old man was self-centred and reclusive. Having fallen out with his wife, he chose to lead a separate life from her, his son and five daughters. As the likely heir to the estate, his only son, Charles, was largely neglected by his father – the latter paying little attention to the boy's education and threatening him with disinheritance every time the young man stepped out of line. For his part, the lad lived a reckless life, complaining often that the allowance he received from his father was insufficient to cover his expenses. And so it was that the distance between father and son became more than just a physical divide.

The trouble started with the younger Drew's choice of partner. He was smitten with the straight-talking Elizabeth Boyer, a woman who seemed ideally suited to Charles and who had made her long term intentions very clear from the outset. In January 1740, when she pressed for them to be married, Charles was overheard by a servant as saying, 'Betsey, let us stay a little longer; it will be worse for us both if I do it now, for my father will certainly disinherit me.' In response, it was claimed that she uttered the fateful line, 'I wish somebody would shoot the old dog.'

Whether this pushed Charles to act, we may never know, but it does seem clear that he began to plan his father's murder shortly after this. His first step was to hire some experienced help. Falling in with some smugglers in Essex, Charles invited Edward Humphreys, a well known local villain, to meet with him at Elizabeth Boyer's lodgings. In return for a large sum of money and the promise of a further £200 a year for life, Humphreys agreed to kill old man Drew.

On the night itself, Charles Drew senior was attended by only one of his staff of servants. He worked alone in his study until midnight when he roused the servant with instructions to deliver a letter the next morning. The servant fell asleep shortly afterwards, oblivious to the events that were to follow.

Edward Humphreys rode up from Witham in Essex to meet the young Charles Drew at around eleven o'clock that night, in a lane close to the Drew estate. Charles already had with him a gun loaded with lead slugs. Humphreys got off his horse and tethered the animal in a nearby field. The two then made for Charles' lodgings, where they took a brandy together, before heading off towards the attorney's townhouse.

It had been agreed that Charles would keep out of sight, while Humphreys was to knock on the door of the house, ask for the elder Drew and then shoot the old man when he appeared. In the event, Humphreys' nerve deserted him at the last moment and he threw down the gun, refusing to go through with the murder. Incensed, Charles picked up the weapon, ordered Humphreys to keep quiet and stay hidden and walked to the door. Prompting the old man to answer, Charles waited for the door to open before shooting his father three times. He then made off from the scene, leaving the door to the street wide open and his father dead on the floor. Incredibly, the shots failed to rouse either the servant or any of the neighbours.

Charles rejoined Humphreys with the announcement that the task had been completed. The two men then walked to nearby Liston Hall before parting company. Humphreys reclaimed his horse and rode to Dunmow in Essex, before heading on to London.

Waking and rising a little before daylight, the manservant in the townhouse found his master's body on the floor, with the door to the street still wide open. Old man Drew's coat was singed and he had three visible bullet holes on his body. There was no sign that anything had been taken from the property and the servant raised the alarm, stunned that he had not been woken during the shooting.

Had it not been for the lengths that Charles Drew went to in trying to conceal his crime, the young firebrand may well have escaped justice. As it transpired, he travelled to London and immediately made an application for a King's pardon for the murderer's accomplice. In those days it was not uncommon for a monarch to grant a pardon to anyone who subsequently provided evidence against a criminal colleague.

Charles' intention was to divert any suspicion away from himself, by pretending to be supporting the murderer's accomplice in coming forward to give evidence against his partner in crime. What Humphreys felt about this strange tactic we may never know, but the pardon was duly granted and on 16th February, through an agent, Charles then offered a reward of £100 to the fictitious accomplice on conviction of the murderer. Luckily for him, Humphreys chose not to take advantage of the offer.

The action served only to heighten the interest of the public and the police. As a known felon, Humphreys was arrested on suspicion and, failing to give a satisfactory account of himself and his whereabouts on the night of the murder, was taken to Bury gaol. In desperation, Charles sent him £20 to secure his silence and promised £100 more for his continued co-operation. But the intelligence that was being gathered on Humphreys convinced the authorities that they had indeed got their man.

Charles next took the unwise step of declaring publicly that Humphreys was not guilty and even threatened to prosecute the police officer who had apprehended the Essex smuggler. Fearing for his own safety, the errant son then headed for London, under the assumed name of Thomas Roberts and tried to keep a low profile.

In an ironic twist of fate, it was another Drew that then pursued the criminals in the early part of March. The unrelated Timothy Drew, another attorney, set out to track Charles down after learning that he was lodging at a private property in Shire Lane. Armed with a magistrate's warrant he searched the house in vain, before following the trail to several locations, and ending up at a property in Leicester Fields. Asking about the whereabouts of a Mr Roberts, the attorney initially drew a blank from the landlord, but suspected that Charles was still lodging in the property. When he threatened to arrest all of the staff for concealing a murderer, he was rewarded with the confession that the younger Drew was indeed still in the house. Charles was seized and delivered into the hands of the local justice of the peace, who interrogated the murderer for six hours before having him committed to Newgate prison.

Desperate to escape the clutches of the law, Charles then tried to bribe Jonathan Keate, the prison warder, or 'turnkey' at Newgate, into releasing him. Requesting that the warder accompany him to France, Charles offered a bond of £1,000 and promised to share half his fortune with the official if he would allow him to abscond. Playing Charles for a fool, the turnkey duly reported the matter to the prison governor, who had the inmate searched and removed to the condemned 'hole'. Here he was watched night and day by prison guards until his trial in late March.

Drew's trial at the Bury Assizes lasted for five hours. At least 16 witnesses were called, with only two being called in his defence. The evidence against him was so overwhelming that the jury found him guilty there and then without retiring to consider their verdict. His punishment was to be death by hanging and he was detained at Bury to await the execution.

In the days following the trial, Charles seemed to play down his guilt. He still blamed his father for the treatment he had suffered and bemoaned the fact that his father had refused to make over an estate to him. His sisters visited him, but avoided talking about the crime, trying only to console him in the last days of his life.

On 9th April 1740, the wayward son was hanged near Bury St Edmunds in front of one of the largest crowds ever seen at a public execution. In his final moments Charles begged the clergyman in attendance to carry on with his prayers, realising perhaps, in those fateful few seconds, the enormity of the crime he had committed against his own flesh and blood.

THE SHINGLE STREET MYSTERY

❖

British wartime conspiracy theories are nothing new. And the fact that the Official Secrets Act continues to prevent a wealth of military and government intelligence from being made public, has fuelled both informed investigations and wild speculation about a variety of events from the Second World War. One such story has been the enduring mystery surrounding an alleged Nazi invasion in August 1940 along a windswept stretch of the Suffolk coastline known as Shingle Street – a tale with all the hallmarks of an official cover-up.

Shingle Street is a row of isolated cottages built along a wide stretch of stones and pebbles which have been thrown up by the sea to form a high bank. The desolate hamlet lies to the south of Orford Ness, and close to the town of Woodbridge, facing the Hollesley Bay. Its historical vulnerability as a point for potential assault is best illustrated by the survival of a Martello tower at the end of the village, which was built in the early 1800s to counter the threat of invasion by Napoleon.

That something happened off the Suffolk coast in the area of Shingle Street on the night of Saturday, 31st August 1940, is not disputed. Ronald Ashford – who has spent many years investigating the story and is firmly convinced that what took place that night was a failed German invasion – was a member of the Local Defence Volunteers at the time. His eye-witness account is both intriguing and compelling.

Ashford recounts how the alarm was raised along the East Suffolk coast and his unit was dug in behind a long brick wall facing the Aldeburgh marshes on that clear, dark evening. He describes how, at around 9.00 pm, 'the heavens appeared to open up south of Orford Lighthouse, in the Shingle Street area', before going on to say, 'We heard a tremendous amount of gunfire and explosions. The night sky was lit up with a red glow. Sporadic gunfire went on for several hours. We received word that a German landing had taken place. This was later confirmed by eye-witness accounts of a shoreline littered with burned bodies.'

Others have told similar tales of a sea of fire and a secret invasion attempt at Shingle Street. And a number of people have come forward to support the assertion that bodies were washed up along the Suffolk coastline. Mike Pantin recalled how his father, a soldier during the war, had been called out to pull dead bodies from the sea off Shingle Street, adding that, 'The common thread to all this was that all these bodies were very badly burned and all were in full German Wermacht uniform ... after being recovered these bodies were removed by army vehicles and all those involved were given very strict orders that this matter was never to be discussed, either at the time or at any time afterwards.'

One resident in nearby Bawdsey, whose garden stretched to the cliffs overlooking the beach at Shingle Street, told friends how he walked to the bottom of his garden that night, saw the sea alight and had been frightened by what he saw. The next day he described seeing bodies all along the beach and soldiers loading corpses onto lorries.

Proponents of the invasion theory have suggested that the Germans wasted no time in planning an assault on Britain following the British defeat at Dunkirk in early 1940. With the British forces severely weakened and a large proportion of the army forced to surrender, it is likely that the country was extremely vulnerable to an attack from across the Channel by the summer of that year.

The story of a German invasion, codenamed Operation Sea Lion, along the Suffolk coast has certainly been a persistent and enduring legend which has inspired numerous works of fiction and a number of authoritative texts, not least of which was Peter Haining's 2004 book *Where the Eagle Landed*. What is certain is that the threat of an enemy attack was taken seriously at the time.

Like other parts of East Anglia, Suffolk was in the front line from the start of the war, with its long, easily accessible, coastline providing a number of suitable landing places for any invasion fleet. In preparation for an anticipated assault, the British authorities installed hundreds of concrete pill boxes and other defences, on and offshore, to repel any invasion attempt. It has also been suggested that the defences at key points, like Shingle Street, included pipelines which ran into the sea, just past the low tide line, to enable combustible liquid to be pumped into the water and ignited. Perhaps it was these defences that accounted for the eye-witness testimonies of a 'sea of fire'.

Alongside Suffolk's vulnerability to invasion, Peter Haining cites the coastline's strategic importance as a testing ground for weapons of mass destruction. Shingle Street is situated right between two establishments, Bawdsey Manor to the south and Orford Ness to the north, both of which played an important part in the war. Bawdsey Manor Radar Station had been in operation since 1936, having run the first successful anti-aircraft radar tests, and was instrumental in defeating the might of the Luftwaffe. Orford Ness was a secret establishment where a lot of weapons testing and simulated attacks were carried out. All of which made Shingle Street an even bigger target for invading forces.

But not everyone is convinced by the invasion theory. Military historian James Hayward, whose book *Shingle Street: The Nazi Invasion that Never Was* was quoted in a *Sunday Express* feature on 17th July 2005, as saying that, 'it didn't happen ... the first stories about something happening

Shingle Street occupies a remote stretch of Suffolk coastline. (Christine Battle)

at Shingle Street were reported in 1971. The stories about a German attack started circulating in the early '90s. It is a story that has kept cropping up every 10 years. There's absolutely no evidence, that's the great problem, there's no history'.

Winston Churchill consistently denied that any invasion attempt had ever taken place in Britain. Similarly, historians have found no evidence in the German archives of any planned or attempted landing at Shingle Street. Despite this, Ronald Ashford is still convinced that what he saw that August night in 1940 was an invasion force of German soldiers who were thwarted in their attempt to reach the shore by the Suffolk coastal defences. In a website dedicated to his conspiracy theory, he maintains that the matter was hushed up, at the highest levels, to prevent further erosion to the already fragile public morale following the defeat at Dunkirk.

In support of his claims, Mr Ashford suggests that there is evidence of a flotilla of small vessels commandeered by the German Army being picked up by radar while crossing the

North Sea that night and of injured and badly burned German survivors arriving in occupied French and Belgian ports in the aftermath of the failed landing attempt. He also claims that the authorities evacuated the residents of Shingle Street and other villages along this stretch of coast prior to the secret invasion, aware of what the Germans had planned.

A number of alternative explanations have also been suggested, including the theory that the events were a British training exercise that went horribly wrong. Another theory is that the Shingle Street story was an attempt to cover up for the loss of lives on a British naval destroyer. A team from BBC East investigated the events of 1940 at Shingle Street for a television programme called 'Inside Out' in 2002. They suggested that the story of a failed Nazi invasion may have been manufactured by Sefton Delmer, head of the Political Warfare Executive, Britain's wartime propaganda unit. There were accounts of a destroyer running into an enemy minefield at the time, while investigating reports of possible invasion barges off the coast of Denmark. Many of the survivors from this vessel were brought ashore on the East Anglian coast and it is thought that the incident was hushed up. The rumours of a failed invasion attempt may therefore have been used for propaganda purposes.

The official documents relating to this incident are due for release in 2021 but whether or not they will tell the full story is debatable. Whatever the real facts, the events at Shingle Street in the summer of 1940 demonstrate how fragile Britain's coastal defences were to enemy invasion. Whether the result of a real invasion attempt, the destruction of a British destroyer or a training exercise gone wrong, the events at Shingle Street were a telling and shocking reminder of the threats faced by Suffolk people in those turbulent years of global conflict.

MEDIEVAL MURDER IN BURY ST EDMUNDS

❖

Bury St Edmunds has a long history, from its earliest roots as a Saxon settlement through to its modern day position as a prosperous centre for brewing, manufacturing and tourism. The fortunes of the Abbey Church of St Edmund, in particular, have been closely intertwined with those of the town and the expansion and prosperity of the settlement in the Middle Ages owed much to the control and patronage of the abbots who resided there. But the period was also marked by darker episodes, including a number of high profile murders, with the abbey often at the centre of events.

It was in the 11th century that King Canute replaced the existing monastery of Bury St Edmunds with an abbey. Two centuries before this, the remains of Edmund, the martyred King of East Anglia (see chapter 10), had been brought to the site giving the town its modern name. As an institution of considerable power and influence, the abbey grew enormously wealthy – at one time owning half of Suffolk – and alongside it Bury thrived as a medieval trading centre and a popular destination for pilgrims, keen to visit the remains of St Edmund.

By the 12th century, the population of the town had reached 4,000 and wool-manufacturing and related crafts had become the mainstay of the local economy. But Bury had also emerged as a major religious and political centre and in 1214 played host to an important meeting of English barons who swore an oath in the abbey to compel the king

Abbey buildings in Bury St Edmunds.

to agree to the terms of Magna Carta. From that time the town has proudly broadcast its motto: 'Shrine of a king, Cradle of the law'.

But the control exerted over the town by the abbot did not always sit well with the local populace. Denied many of the freedoms available to other boroughs not under the control of a monastery or abbey, the people of Bury rioted for three days in 1327. About 3,000 protestors stormed the abbey gates, attacking the inhabitants and damaging many of its buildings. They also blocked all roads to London and threw about 20 monks into gaol.

The abbot then went back on an agreement he had made with the citizens and they raided the abbey again. The rioting continued for most of the year and when the monks organised a counter-attack on the congregation of a local church, the monastery was nearly destroyed in the violence which followed, fuelling the mayhem.

The period of civil unrest continued sporadically into the following year with the mob still demanding a charter to enable them to govern their own affairs. This period of unrest was temporarily halted by the intervention of the Sheriff of Norfolk, Robert Morley. The culprits were brought to justice and fined the substantial sum of £14,000. Even after the fine, many of the town's burgesses were reluctant to concede. They were all too ready to join forces with the outlaw gang led by Thomas Thornham and make their protests known.

After taking up residence at Moyse's Hall, Thornham and his followers managed to avoid arrest before audaciously kidnapping the abbot and smuggling him to London. A contemporary tract called 'Depraedatio Abbatiae Sancti Edmundi' describes the extraordinary events surrounding the kidnapping of the abbot and gives it a rather supernatural twist. 'After this about midnight on St Helen's Day, in the same year (August 18th, 1328) came Thomas de Thornham with many fugitives and outlaws into the town of St Edmund, and by force siezed the keys of all the gates of the town, and none of the townsmen saying them nay, hurried off to breakfast at Moyse's Hall, and on their way killed Roger Peasenhall, a servant of the abbey. And the men of the town being full of joy at their coming, celebrated this breakfast by the many gifts they made towards it.

'But one thing happened there which might have struck fear into them. For when a woman out of Cook's Street had come to take the price of the meal she had sold them she looked into the cellar close to them, and saw a most horrible devil, as though he were writing. And all of a tremble at his horrible countenance, she drew back the foot which she had put across the threshold, but not without punishment, for instantly, that foot was roasted by infernal fire, and fell rotting from her body.'

The meaning of this account we shall never know but we do know that the abbot was moved from town to town in an attempt to confuse the authorities. But by 1329, the abductors were excommunicated and some had been brought to justice. The abbot returned to his home later that year and yet another £14,000 fine was imposed on the town. It wasn't until 1331 that a peace treaty was drawn up and matters were truly laid to rest.

In 1349, the town entered another dark period when it was devastated by the impact of the black death – the disease killing off as much as half of the population of the town, which in turn left farms and stock untended. There was little production and established markets were decimated.

Events in 1369 brought further, unwanted, attention to the Abbey with a murder mystery involving three monks, John de Norton, John de Grafton and William Blundeston, who fell out with each other. It was alleged that Grafton stabbed Norton to death one night while the abbey slept. Fearing repercussions he attempted to cover up the scandal, aided by William Blundeston, by burying Norton in a shallow grave. But Abbot John de Brinkley discovered the body and exposed the culprits, imprisoning the men for the crime.

In the event, the king pardoned both monks without trial, declaring that the crime had taken place in 'hot blood', a judgement peculiar to the period and illustrating the power and influence of the church at that time and the importance of royal patronage.

The Peasants' Revolt of 1381 brought more upheaval to the town and abbey and further, high profile, murders. As the uprising gained momentum, the people of Bury were ready to do battle once again. The monks had already fled, however and, as there was no abbot in place, the peasants were free to loot the abbey unopposed. They also captured the prior and chief justice, murdered them and stuck their heads on poles in the town centre for all to see. The episode did little to cement relations with the monarchy and it took a year longer than everywhere else in England for the town and abbey to be readmitted to the King's Peace.

Alongside these earlier episodes of medieval murder and mayhem, Bury St Edmunds was also the setting for another strange murder mystery in 1447. In that year, King Henry VI called for his Parliament to sit in Bury in the Great Refectory. Humphrey, Duke of Gloucester was summoned at short notice to appear before the House, charged with high treason. It was no secret that Henry and his wife Queen Margaret viewed the duke with suspicion as a political enemy.

Humphrey was lodged in St Saviours, outside the north Gate of the town. The charges against him were real enough, but his unexpected death five days later, attributed to a stroke brought on by the shock of the events, had all the hallmarks of a murder and cover up. So much so, that William Shakespeare was later to refer to the incident in Part II, Act III of his play, 'Henry VI'.

One persistent legend has it that Humphrey was murdered by Maude Carew, a lady of the royal court and a loyal friend to Queen Margaret. She is alleged to have despatched the duke by poisoning the door handle of his bedroom. Having confessed her crime to a priest, she was apparently cursed and as the 'grey lady' is believed by some to haunt the ruins of St Mary's churchyard on the night of 24th February each year, racked by the guilt of her crime.

Bury St Edmunds continued to have a rich and turbulent history well beyond the middle ages, but those early years provide a vivid illustration of the upheavals caused by the often fragile balance of power between the Church, the aristocracy and the wider body of local citizens.

SUFFOLK'S BIG CATS

───────────── ❀ ─────────────

East Anglia has no shortage of fascinating and ghoulish tales about the appearance of devil dogs and hell hounds. In fact the legend of Black Shuck, the hell-hound which stalks East Anglia and is said to bring death within the year to anyone who dares look into its flaming eyes, is firmly rooted in local folklore. What is less well known is that the region is also a popular area for sightings of big cats and in recent years many of these have been reported in Suffolk.

According to the British Big Cats Society (BBCS), which was set up 'To Prove and to Protect' the existence of exotic wild cats, there are over 1,000 reported sightings of pumas, leopards, panthers and other wild beasts in Britain each year. Some 60 to 70 per cent of these are of large black felines. It is believed that many of these creatures were released into the wild after 1976 when the Dangerous Wild Animals Act was introduced and may have bred.

Danny Bampling, a founder member and spokesman for the BBCS, was quoted in 2003 as saying that, 'Suffolk is a rural area in which people were likely to have private collections of these animals up to and after 1976.' He added that, 'Cats wish to remain elusive and so the sightings are rare and short-lived, but I have no doubt that there are such cats in Suffolk.'

An intriguing case in East Suffolk concerned the so-called 'Beccles Lynx'. The *Eastern Daily Press* newspaper reported in January 2003 that a 59-pound Northern lynx had been shot near the town in 1991 by a local farmer. He had

Eastern Daily Press, **Thursday,** March 16, 2006

REPORT: Big cat society backs 'Beccles lynx'

Controversy over wild cat-alogue

By LORNA MARSH

Nearly 150 sightings of big cats roaming the Norfolk, Suffolk and Cambridgeshire countryside were reported in just 15 months, according to startling figures released yesterday.

And the research, carried out by the British Big Cats Society (BBCS), suggests reported sightings are increasing.

The BBCS report, to be published in the April issue of BBC Wildlife magazine, reveals that 2123 sightings of big cats in Britain were reported between April 2004 and last July.

Out of those, 54 were in Norfolk, 60 in Suffolk and 34 in Cambridgeshire. Details of exact locations were unavailable.

The article follows several high-profile reports of big cats in the region and makes reference to what has become known as the Beccles lynx, which many believe to be a hoax.

As reported by the EDP, a photograph of what appears to be a Northern lynx, shot by a farmer in 1991 near the town, surfaced in 2003 on the BBCS website.

In the BBC Wildlife magazine, BBCS founder Danny Bamping maintains the photo is genuine and that the 59lb adult cat had killed 15 sheep in two weeks.

However Mr Bamping says he has uncovered several

MYSTERY MOGGIE: A lynx which was reportedly found at Beccles.

"hoaxes", including a photo of a supposed black panther in Wales printed by two national tabloids last April that turned out to be a full-size black stuffed toy.

Mr Bamping said: "This is a good example of how easy it is to produce a hoax.

"This year we have been able to study evidence in greater detail and estimate that just under a third of all reported sightings are not big cats – either people have been mistaken or their reports are too vague.

"There are also those people who insist on reporting the likes of the Pink Panther, Garfield, Top Cat and Simba."

Sophie Stafford, editor of BBC Wildlife magazine, said: "With fresh new evidence and sightings on the increase, the

British Big Cats Society is now tantalisingly close to being able to provide conclusive proof of their presence."

The BBCS hopes for national support, in particular the police and the Department for the Enviroment, Food and Rural Affairs (Defra), saying some regional police forces are taking a keen interest.

In Norfolk, dedicated wildlife officers deal with any reported sightings within their designated areas.

But a Defra spokesman said it did not believe big cats were living in the wild in England.

The South West was the top region for sightings, with Devon the number one county on 132 sightings. Cornwall and Somerset were in the top 10. Scotland came in third with Wales fourth.

Press clipping of the alleged shooting in 1991 of the 'Beccles Lynx'. (Eastern Daily Press)

apparently despatched the creature after 15 of his sheep had been killed in a two week period.

The story only emerged after a photograph of the alleged lynx appeared on the BBCS website. The newspaper further reported that the dead cat had been stored in the farmer's freezer for some time until it was sold on to a game dealer who had it stuffed. Fearful of the legal ramifications of killing a wild animal, the characters involved had sought to keep the story quiet.

Whilst trumpeted by some as proof that big cats really do exist in Suffolk, there were many in the local hunting fraternity who cast doubt on the authenticity of this particular story.

That aside, sightings of big cats have occurred in all parts of the county in the last decade. Throughout 1996 there was a wave of reported sightings in and around the Ipswich area, including one on the main A12 by-pass and another along Kelly Road. On the Tuddenham Road, close to a pet cemetery, a car full of people saw what they described as a cat the size of a tiger with a jet black coat.

A Beccles couple, walking their dog in Dunwich forest in September 1998, came across a large paw print, which they believed to be that of a big cat. The photograph they took confirms that it is indeed substantial enough to belong to a large feline and, with no visible imprint of claw marks, is unlikely to be a dog – cats being able to retract their claws. Shortly after taking the photograph, the couple sat down in the woods to enjoy a picnic, but were aware of a strange and unsettling noise nearby, which they described as being 'a cross between a low growl, interspersed with panting'. Unable to see what the creature was and concerned that their dog was visibly terrified by the encounter, the couple beat a hasty retreat back to their car.

More recently, in February 2003, the *Ipswich Evening Star* reported that a woman in Bedfield, near Framlingham, had discovered large paw prints in the snow covering her garden

Paw print of a large cat discovered in Dunwich Forest in 1998.

one morning and was convinced she had earlier seen a large black cat from her bedroom window. The distinct paw prints were about 15 centimetres long and the tracks showed that the animal had come close to the woman's house in the direction of a bird-table, presumably in search of food.

Later that year, the same newspaper carried stories of further black cat sightings. Mike Jennings of Kelsale, reported seeing a large feline while out shooting in Great Livermere, near Bury St Edmunds. He described it as being, 'the size of an Alsatian, maybe a bit bigger'. June Fooks, of Eyke, near Woodbridge, claimed to have seen a similar animal, larger than her pet Labrador, prowling in her garden. She described the cat as having, 'a really shiny coat and a long tail'.

Other sightings have been reported close to Woodbridge. In February 2004, a man walking his dog through

Rendlesham Forest at dusk saw what he thought was a large black cat. Anne Downing, a neighbour to June Fooks in Eyke, also claimed to have seen a similar animal in the area.

That these animals could exist and move around freely, largely without detection, is quite possible. The large, rural and wooded landscape across many parts of Suffolk is ideal for big cats which can cover up to 30 kilometres in a single night.

In May 2004, BBC news reported that a lorry driver had spotted a large black cat walking along a main road in Linstead Parva, near Halesworth. The driver, Martin Emery, said that the animal was about five feet long and four feet high. He believed it to be a panther and claimed that he had seen a paw print nearby.

The BBC carried another story about a big cat sighting in August of that year. Two young anglers claimed to have come within 20 yards of a black, puma-like, creature as they were fishing near Bungay one evening. The eldest of the two brothers described the cat's tail as 'about three feet long', adding that the shape of its head 'was like a house cat's but about five times bigger'. The creature had apparently taken a few steps towards them before making off.

Two weeks later a learner driver from Lowestoft reported seeing a similar creature near Loddon, some six miles from Bungay. Sue Bidwell had been driving between the town and nearby Langley when her husband asked her to pull over. Speaking later to the *Waveney Advertiser* she said, 'As I looked across to my right we saw this big black cat about 300 yards away. It looked like a puma.' She added, 'We could see its long body, big head and long tail above the grass, which was a good two to three feet high.'

Currently there are between 20 and 30 reported sightings of big cats in Suffolk each year. The BBCS believes that for every one of these, another two or three go unreported. If this is the case, there could be more evidence for the existence of big cats in Suffolk than we imagine. Who knows, perhaps Black Shuck was a cat after all?

THE EXECUTION OF
SARAH LLOYD

❁

Like many young women in 19th century Suffolk, Sarah Lloyd chose domestic service as a way of escaping the monotony and rigours of agricultural work. As a maidservant, the 22 year old from Naughton became a reliable and trusted employee of a Mrs Sara Syers of Benton Street, Hadleigh, who regarded her services highly. How sad it was then that this impressionable young maid should fall in love with local plumber and glazier Joseph Clarke, who would persuade her to conspire with him in robbing her mistress in October 1799. And how tragic it was that young Sarah should be executed for her part in a crime that caught the attention of both the local and national press.

Sarah Lloyd was a pretty, quiet natured, girl who chose the wrong man to fall in love with. Describing the woman after her trial, one commentator of the time said, 'her countenance was very pleasing, of a meek and modest expression, perfectly characteristic of a mild and affectionate temper. She had large eyes and eyelids, a short and well formed nose, an open forehead, of a grand and ingenious character, and very regular and pleasing features; her hair darkish brown, and her eyebrows rather darker than her hair ... she had an uncommon and unaffected sweetness in her voice and manner'.

Sarah was seduced by Joseph Clarke, the son of a respectable and influential tradesman. He repeatedly visited Sarah at night in the Benton Street townhouse and continually promised her marriage. There can be little doubt that the young woman was besotted by Clarke and trusted him implicitly.

On the night of 3rd October 1799, Clarke again talked of marriage and persuaded Sarah to assist him in stealing a large number of her mistress's trinkets, an expensive pocket watch and ten gold guinea coins. Not content with the robbery, Clarke set fire to the house to cover his tracks and told Sarah to hide at her mother's home. If apprehended, she was instructed to blame the crime on passing soldiers.

The fire in the house developed rapidly but was eventually brought under control by neighbours. Investigations the following morning revealed the full extent of the damage, the long list of missing items and the absent maid servant.

Sarah was very quickly arrested at her mother's house and charged with burglary and arson. Inept and ill-prepared for a life of crime, Sarah had hidden many of the stolen items in the house. She was taken to the gaol at Bury St Edmunds, where she repeatedly claimed that Clarke had put her up to the robbery.

The trial at the Bury Assizes began in March 1800. The charge of arson was not tried due to a lack of evidence and, despite Sarah's protestations, the case against Clarke faltered for similar reasons and he was acquitted of the burglary.

Sarah was not so fortunate. Whilst also acquitted of the burglary, she was found guilty of capital larceny to the value of 40 shillings – a crime that carried the death penalty. Sentencing her, the judge, Sir Nash Grose, outlined the seriousness of her misdemeanour, declaring that she had betrayed the essential bond of trust between a mistress and servant. She was duly sentenced to be hanged.

A considerable campaign of protest was launched locally and nationally to save Sarah from the hangman's noose. The Rector of Hadleigh, the Reverend Hay Drummond, led the efforts locally, circulating his own petition. This was signed by many of the local gentry, including Mrs Sara Syers, the wronged mistress. She stated that until the crime Sarah's conduct had been exemplary.

In spite of the petition for mercy, the judge reported adversely and the Home Secretary felt there was no reason to ask the king for clemency. The date of execution was set for 9th April 1800.

Reverend Drummond also asked Capel Lofft to assist in the campaign. Lofft was the son of the duchess of Marlborough's private secretary and, as a young barrister and literary figure, was well regarded in London society. He had also served on the Grand Jury which had passed the indictments against Sarah and had sat through the trial, being sympathetic to her case. In readily taking up the cause, he met with Sarah in the condemned cell at Bury gaol and from then on interested himself in the case to an extent which bordered on obsession.

The Prison Governor John Orridge was also sympathetic to Sarah's plight and when he received a stay of execution for one S. Hop, a name unknown to him, he assumed it was for S. Lloyd and used it to delay the date of execution. This gave Lofft further time to appeal to the home secretary for support but it fell on deaf ears and a date was set.

The execution took place on the morning of 23rd April in the pouring rain. Sarah was dressed in a white dress, trimmed with black ribbons – a picture of innocence. Lofft accompanied Sarah in the cart ride to the gallows, comforting her and sheltering her from the rain with his umbrella. He even climbed onto the scaffold to stand beside her, speaking to the crowd and deploring the home secretary's failure to ask the king for clemency.

Throughout his speech, Sarah wept, as did the assembled crowd. But at the fateful moment of execution, Sarah regained her composure, assisting the hangman by holding back her hair as he tightened the noose around her neck. Her last words were, 'I hope I shall be an example to all.' A thousand people turned out at the funeral in Bury St

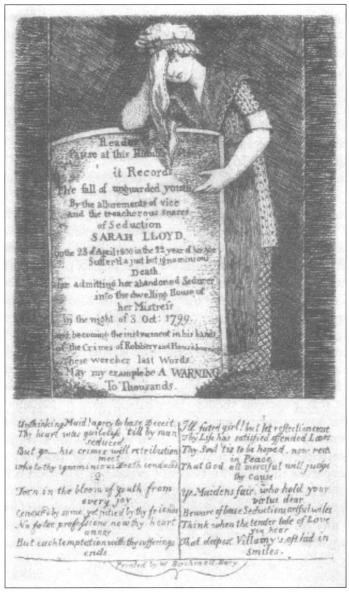

*A local pamphlet produced on the case of Sarah Lloyd after
her execution.* (Suffolk Record Office)

Edmunds that evening, to hear Lofft remind them that she was an 'unfortunate sufferer'.

A tragic consequence of Sarah's execution was her own mother's suicide. On hearing the news that her daughter had breathed her last, the unfortunate woman immediately hanged herself. Neither did Capel Lofft escape unscathed. As a result of his vigorous defence of Sarah and scathing attack on the home secretary's judgement, Lofft was sacked as a magistrate.

Sarah was one of seven women executed that year. That she was indeed a wronged woman is now clear. Upon his release, Joseph Clarke joined the army for a posting in the East Indies. Before his death from a fever in 1802, he freely confessed to the crimes in Hadleigh and his use of the innocent Sarah to gain access to the property.

A pamphlet published locally after the execution said the case illustrated, '... the importance of sobriety, chastity, fidelity, honesty, obedience... She first fell a victim to seduction. She lost her virtue, her sense of rectitude, and her life'.

Sarah's tombstone in the churchyard of Charnel House in Bury St Edmunds echoes this sentiment: 'Reader, pause at this humble stone. It records the fall of unguarded youth by the allurement of vice and the treacherous snares of seduction.' Another pamphlet, published at the time by a local printer under the heading, 'The Warning of Sarah Lloyd', shows a picture of the young maidservant looking over the tombstone, with a verse addressed to other girls about the perils of seduction. It serves as a pithy reminder of the tragedy of Sarah Lloyd.

SAINT EDMUND –
MARTYRED KING OF
EAST ANGLIA

In the aftermath of the Roman invasion of Britain, it was to be the Germanic tribes of the Angles, Saxons, Frisians and Jutes that became the lifeblood of the East Anglian population, colonising large areas, establishing new settlements and cultivating the land. In their wake, the Vikings brought further influences to the cultural diversity of the 'East Angles', but not without fierce hostility from the incumbent tribes. As an independent kingdom, East Anglia was ruled at this time by a young, unmarried king in his late twenties. And who better to rule and defend the vulnerable coastline than Edmund, a compassionate king whose Old English name meant 'noble protection', and whose reputation as a man of incomparable size and stature was legendary? The story of Edmund's resistance to the Vikings, his ultimate demise and later veneration as a Christian martyr is a story well established in Suffolk history, but it is also a tale of mystery, miracles and mythology.

The Vikings may have been peace-loving in their Scandinavian heartlands, but were one of many wandering tribes that were unable to curb their bloodlust when travelling overseas. And facing their lands back home, it was East Anglia that was to suffer most at the hands of the marauding Danes. In the late ninth century, the heathen warriors wreaked havoc on the Christian population, destroying churches and monasteries and levelling homes and villages. By the autumn of AD 869, the large Viking army had established its winter quarters in Norfolk, led by the fearsome Ivar 'the Boneless'.

Edmund faced overwhelming odds in defending his lands against this army. Urging his men to take up arms and to fight for the honour of their faith and country, Edmund led them into battle near Thetford, during which both sides suffered severe losses, until the whole field was red with the blood of the slain. Although the Viking army withdrew at the end of the day, Edmund vowed never to fight them in battle again and to sacrifice his life if necessary to preserve his nation. He had but a short time to wait, as Ivar was soon joined at Thetford by Ubbi, his brother, and 10,000 extra men, all intent on revenge.

King Edmund and his followers re-established their dishevelled army in the village of Hoxne in Suffolk, but were eventually surrounded by Ivar's men, The Norsemen offered Edmund a deal; to become a puppet-king under heathen rule or to die. Refusing steadfastly to renounce his Christian faith, Edmund chose death. On 20th November – now worshiped as Saint Edmund's day – the Vikings bound the king, whipped and beat him with clubs and tied him to an oak tree. They then fired countless arrows at him before beheading the brave leader.

Throughout the remainder of the winter the Vikings continued to plunder Edmund's lands until the following spring, when they set sail for home. Edmund's body had been left unburied during this time and his severed head discarded in thick brambles. Folklore tells how some local men discovered the body and were drawn to the hidden head by a mysterious voice which answered their desperate cries. The head was discovered in thorn bushes, watched over by a grey wolfhound, possibly Edmund's own loyal hunting dog. When the men took Edmund's remains back to Hoxne, the wolfhound followed them to the edge of the village, but then retreated back into the trees. The body and head were laid to rest in a hastily constructed chapel.

From those early days of his burial, Edmund was held in awe by local people and legend has it that miracles began to occur around his place of rest. Sick and blind people were healed and a light was seen over his tomb. When the remains were unearthed to be reburied in a large church in the royal village of Beodericsworth (renamed Bury St Edmunds), the exhumed body was found to be intact, with only a small red scar indicating where the head had been severed. From that point on, Edmund's relics became a site of pilgrimage for Christians from across Europe.

In the 10th century, Edmund was declared the first Patron Saint of England, and any mention of his name would be greeted with cries of 'For England and for Freedom'. The cult of St Edmund continued, as did the stories about the magical powers his bones appeared to possess. In 1211, during the Fourth Crusade, a captured mosque in the city of Damietta, in the Nile delta, was re-dedicated to St Edmund when a stone fell out of the roof of the building and killed a man who had mocked the saint.

In the early part of the 13th century, St Edmund's relics were stolen by French knights and transported to the great abbey in Toulouse, France. The abbey was completely destroyed in the 16th century, but it was not until the beginning of the 20th century that most of the relics were returned to England, to be concealed and housed safely in a Catholic church at Arundel in Sussex. A small number of the Saint's bones were re-housed in the church at Bury St Edmunds during the 1960s.

The story of Edmund's murder at Hoxne was given greater credence in the 19th century, when the oak tree which believers claimed he had been tied to over a thousand years before, fell to the ground. When sawn up, the tree was found to contain a Danish arrowhead – evidence perhaps of the torture inflicted on the martyred king.

The enigma of St Edmund was not confined to the miracles claimed by his worshipers. When he became known as the Patron Saint of East Anglia, Edmund's symbol was of three crowns, representing his martyrdom, his kingship and his virginity. Legend has it that three actual crowns were produced after the Norman Conquest, in honour of St Edmund, and that these were buried in secrecy around the coastline to protect England from the threat of invasion. According to local folklore, one of these crowns was lost to the waves when the town of Dunwich fell into the sea. A second was dug up at Rendlesham in the 17th century and melted down for its silver content. The final crown is said to remain buried in its secret location.

True or not, the mystery surrounding the holy crowns, and the story of St Edmund himself, bears an uncanny similarity to the legend of Bran, the giant king of Britain, who was one of the chief gods of the Celts. In Celtic mythology, he was a giant whose stride spanned the sea and who was seen as a strong and generous king. The name 'Bran' is thought to derive from the Celtic warrior Brennos, who led an early invasion of Macedonia during the period 282 to 280 BC with 30,000 men, although the Celtic word Bran also means 'Raven', the bird most closely associated with the god.

Bran is portrayed in the 'Romance of Branwen', a tale contained in the *Mabinogion* – an assembly of Welsh stories about people in Celtic times. In the story, Bran is mortally wounded by a poison dart. He tells his companions to cut off his head and to take it across the sea 'and bear it even unto the White Mount, in London, and bury it there, with the face towards France'. His companions carry the head across the sea and in their travels they feast for 80 years with the severed head entertaining them, as the giant king once did. During this time they have no cares and all their sorrows are forgotten. When the feast ends, they carry his head to London and bury it under the White Mount, the site of Tower Hill where the Tower of London now stands. Alongside the tradition that if the ever-present ravens should leave, the Tower of London would crumble and a great disaster would befall Britain, the legend of Bran has it that the buried head will protect Britain from invasion.

The local connection with the Celtic god Bran may be reflected in the Romano British shore fort of Branodunum, the 'Fortress of Bran', in north Norfolk, on which site lies the modern town of Brancaster, although other settlements also reflect the name. In Norfolk, there is Brandiston and Brandon Parva, while Suffolk can claim Brandon, Brandeston and Brantham. Further south, there is also the village of Bran End in Essex.

Whatever the parallels between the legends of St Edmund and Bran, it is the former that continues to be most closely associated with the history of Suffolk, East Anglia and England. Perhaps it is no surprise then that his symbol features on the East Anglian flag, the three holy crowns shown against the backdrop of the English national flag, a standard that proclaims the importance of this unyielding and revered East Anglian ruler.

THE WILFUL MURDER OF
MRS PHILIPS

❁

It is often said that there is no honour among thieves. This was certainly true when a gang of villains set out to rob a Mrs Philips in the sleepy village of Eriswell, in the west of Suffolk, in October 1782. Their ill-conceived crime would lead two of the men to the gallows and the unfortunate Mrs Philips to an early grave.

James May, Jeremiah Theobald and the brothers Henry and Benjamin Wiseman were no strangers to crime. Along with a character named Munsell, they had form for a number of petty crimes in and around the Mildenhall area. Theobald had been tried at the most recent Lent Assizes for robbing the home of a Mr Fuller in Melford. Having been found guilty of the crime he had been permitted to enlist as a soldier. He and May were also under suspicion for horse-stealing from a gentleman in Boxwell – the horse in question having been found in a field next to May's farm in Mildenhall.

The gang's in-fighting began before the crime against Mrs Philips had even taken place. Munsell had provided the intelligence on Mrs Philips, suggesting to the others, more than once, that the woman was extremely wealthy and would be easy to rob. But when they decided on a night for the crime, Munsell refused to join the others.

As it turned out, Mrs Philips was anything but easy to rob. The four men forced their way into the home at Eriswell on the chosen night, disturbing the lady of the house and systematically plundering the property of anything they could usefully carry off. Mrs Philips began to fight and scream to such an extent that May and Benjamin Wiseman were forced to restrain her, telling her to keep quiet and initially putting her down in the cellar of the house. When her protests continued, the two men brought her up from the cellar, placed a sack over her head and carried her out and into a field not far from the house. Wiseman held her by the throat to prevent her making any further noise. May then left him to rejoin the others.

Benjamin Wiseman's rough handling proved too much for Mrs Philips who was left on the ground, lifeless and covered in the sack, about a quarter of a mile from her home. None of the gang had planned to kill, so we can imagine their horror at finding out what Wiseman had done. To add to their troubles, the criminals also believed that they had looted less than they hoped for and no more than six or seven pounds in cash. In reality, their haul of trinkets and money was later valued at around £150.

Henry Wiseman, clearly the fence for the gang, took charge of the most valuable items which included a number of rings. The remaining cash was divided up between the four, who decided to go their separate ways and keep a low profile. Wiseman later attempted to sell at least one diamond ring to a Jew named Samuel, but the dealer refused to touch the stolen property.

The gang's attempts to lie low were unsuccessful and within a few days May and Theobald had been arrested for the robbery and murder of Mrs Philips. Munsell was also arrested, but fearing the noose for his earlier involvement in planning the crime, collaborated with the authorities against his two former colleagues. The prisoners were transported to Bury gaol to await trial.

On 14th November 1782, May and Theobald were taken by horse-drawn cart to the Bury Assizes for a pre-trial hearing. Confronted with the sight of Munsell, Theobald shouted out, 'Damn you Munsell, I am sure of death, but you shall not live so long.' Taking the threat seriously, the authorities arranged for Munsell to be held in the Mildenhall Bridewell for his own protection until the trial had taken place.

The trial of James May and Jeremiah Theobald was held on 26th March 1783. Both were sentenced to death for the murder of Mrs Philips. A few days later they faced the executioner and were hanged for the crime. Both had continued to protest their innocence of the actual murder. The hanging attracted a huge amount of public attention at the time, the printed broadsheet of the trial and execution selling in large numbers when it was published on 12th April 1783 at a price of six pence.

Less than six months later, Benjamin Wiseman was arrested and sentenced to two years' imprisonment for receiving some stolen goods belonging to a Dr Bate in Freckenham. During the process, he confessed to the murder of Mrs Philips, but no further action was taken against him as May and Theobald had already been found guilty and executed for the crime. Henry Wiseman, for his part, appears to have evaded any punishment for the crime in Eriswell.

Had it not been for the evidence presented by Munsell, there is a possibility that May and Theobald may also have escaped justice as they had so many times in their earlier criminal careers. And as the original architect of the robbery, Munsell must have thanked his lucky stars that he too had not faced the hangman's gibbet on that fateful day in March 1783.

GHOSTLY TALES FROM IPSWICH

❖

As the county town of Suffolk, Ipswich has an extensive history and is in fact the longest continuously occupied town in England. Starting life as a small Saxon trading settlement in the early seventh century, 'Gippa's Wic' or 'Gip's Wic', soon developed into a flourishing port with trade links to Germany and many other parts of Europe. The wool trade, in particular, provided a good living for local farmers, textile workers, merchants and sailors. But the town also has a rich vein of stories and folklore about the phantoms, ghouls and poltergeists that appear to haunt many of its buildings – each having its own particular story to tell.

Most reported sightings of the supernatural have been in the centre of Ipswich, a fair number concentrated around the Buttermarket shopping area. Betty Puttick, in her book, *Ghosts of Suffolk*, tells of a phantom monk seen by workers at a former factory on the site belonging to W. S. Cowell and Company, which was built over the ruins of an old monastery. Others have reported similar apparitions and the sound of ghostly footsteps in the factory before it was demolished.

The sighting of monks and friars is widely reported across the central area of the town and may be linked to the original plot of land granted to the Black Friars in 1348 which, with later extensions to the site, ran from

The Halberd Inn, allegedly haunted by the spirit of a murdered monk.

St Margaret's Plain, near Christchurch Park in the north, to Star Lane in the south, and west to east from the old town wall to Foundation Street. Perhaps it is no surprise that the area plays host to a popular local attraction known as the 'Black Friars Ghost Walk'.

This theory is also supported by the sightings of a monk in a nearby public house. P. J. McGinty & Sons in the Halberd Inn building on Northgate Street is allegedly haunted by the ghost of a monk who was murdered and thrown down an indoor well. Tales abound of poltergeist activity in the property, including one story about all of the fuses being switched off in a junction box, saving the landlord from electrocution. So at least it is a friendly ghost! An even more bizarre tale has it that, if you place an ear to one of the pub's walls, you can hear a human heartbeat.

The existing manageress of the pub confirmed that she had seen no religious phantoms, but did know of a number of strange incidents that had occurred, including unexplained footsteps in the corridor leading to the pub's toilets and gaskets being turned off in the cellar for no apparent reason. On another occasion, a light bulb fell out of a socket one night but failed to break.

Further tales of poltergeist activity have been reported close to this, in the town's historic Ancient House, by staff working for the kitchen goods firm Lakeland Plastics. From the spring of 1997 staff began to notice odd things happening to their window displays. Flowers arranged for St Valentine's Day were found to have been removed and rearranged on a door mat. Similar disruption occurred on Mother's Day. One member of staff was trapped in a cellar when a door stuck fast. Elsewhere, goods and books began to fall off shelves without reason. In the end, a medium was called in and claimed to be picking up the name 'Lakeland'. A local writer following this up afterwards put forward the theory that the haunting could be related to the Ipswich

The Tourist Information Centre on St Stephen's Lane, where there have been sightings of a female ghost.

woman Mary Lakeland who was tried and burnt for witchcraft in 1645 (see chapter 4).

Nearby, on St Stephen's Lane, the Tourist Information Office is reputed to be haunted by a female ghost. She is believed to be the former organist from the now deconsecrated church of St Stephen's which was renovated for its current role. It is said that she is one of two sisters who campaigned strongly for the church to be saved and who were disappointed when it was declared officially redundant in 1975.

The current manager of the office acknowledged that he had not seen or experienced anything out of the ordinary himself, but did confirm that some members of his staff had felt a presence in the building from time to time. How much of this is merely the result of the high-ceilinged, gothic interior, we may never know, but the structure certainly creates an awe-inspiring atmosphere. When operational, the church was once used for performances of T. S. Eliot's 'Murder in the Cathedral' for this very reason.

A little further north, and still in the centre of the town, is the Great White Horse Hotel on Tavern Street, where it is claimed that the ghost of a 'grey lady' can be seen walking through a wall. Some have linked this to a fire which occurred at some point in the hotel's history.

Within a stone's throw of this, and adjoining Tavern Street, we have Tower Street and the site of The Rep public house. Actors from the original theatre which was based here claimed that the premises were haunted by a spirit known as 'Alfred', his occasional visits being considered by the players to be a sign of good luck. The uninvited spectator would apparently sit silently watching performances in the fourth or fifth row of the theatre.

South-east of this, along Eagle Street, there were reports of poltergeist activity in a private dwelling during the 1950s. The story was that an unknown force had thrown items around the property and scattered a strange powder in the rooms of the house until a local vicar had been called in to perform an exorcism.

In the north east corner of the town another private home was said to have experienced its fair share of paranormal activity. Reports in the 1960s suggested that the home in Waterford Road was haunted by the ghost of a small child in a nightdress. The sightings were accompanied by unexplained noises and footsteps in the upper part of the

The Rep public house – a former theatre and apparently haunted by a ghost named Alfred.

house and accounts of a strange mist travelling between the rooms.

No less intriguing are the recurring sightings of an unearthly 'white lady' in the upstairs rooms of Gippeswyk Hall, which sits on an avenue of the same name. The manifestation apparently occurs on nights of the full moon. One observer claimed also to have seen a ghostly mist rising from the chimney of the property, although no fires were lit at the time.

Equally uncanny were the claims made in the late 1990s by a woman living on Skylark Lane, to the west of the Chantry Estate. Looking down from her landing one night, she saw what she thought was a slim old man dressed in a suit holding on to the banister below. No explanations were given for the unexpected visitor.

The Old Neptune Inn on Fore Street at the back of the Neptune Dock is said to be home to a seafaring spirit known as 'Fred'. The property was once owned by a rich merchant and as a modern holiday home now has 20 splendidly refurbished guest rooms. One of these, the aptly named 'Galleon' room, was restored in the mid-1900s when the room's leaning walls were lined with 19th century wooden printer's blocks and its original angled windows were restored to resemble those of a ship from a bygone age.

Legend has it that 'Fred', a seaman in the 17th century, was hanged in the courtyard for smuggling, and now sits on the bed in the Galleon in full period naval uniform and keeps male guests awake with his incomprehensible chatter. Some nights he walks up and down, swaying from side to side – the result of too much liquor perhaps or maybe the swell of rough seas. As the building is also believed to have once been a smuggler's den, some have claimed that old Fred is a former rum-runner known as 'Admiral Grog'. The room certainly has some provenance, as it was used as a counting house in the days when high water barges off-loaded on the ground floor from a now filled-in creek.

One Ipswich building has a number of supernatural stories attributed to it. Christchurch Mansion is a red brick Tudor house set within the leafy splendour of Christchurch Park. It is built on the site of a 12th-century Augustinian priory, which suffered at the hands of Thomas Cromwell, who ransacked it during Henry VIII's dissolution of the monasteries in 1528.

Today the property is home to a fine collection of art and period furniture, including paintings by the Suffolk artists Gainsborough and Constable. Some have claimed that the pictures on the walls of the mansion mysteriously turn themselves around.

In her book of local ghost stories, Betty Puttick tells of poltergeist activity within the mansion and sightings of a young lady with a bonnet, dressed in white, moving from

The Old Neptune Inn – a bedroom is said to be home to a spirit called Fred.

one of the bedrooms to the parlour of the property. One woman and her daughter claimed to have watched a Victorian woman walk past them and pass through a glass door. The woman is believed by some to be the spirit of a former maid who suffered at the hands of her unscrupulous employer.

In other parts of Ipswich there are equally intriguing tales of the unexplained that chill the senses and challenge beliefs. Real or illusory these stories contribute much to the cultural and historical heritage of the town. And fact or fiction, they fascinate, thrill and entertain us in equal measure.

THE PASSION OF LOVERS

———————❀———————

To say that Ann Beddingfield and Richard Ringe were ill-prepared and ill-equipped to carry out murder would be an understatement. That they succeeded in doing so proved to be the fatal undoing of these two young Suffolk lovers. Some say that love is blind. It certainly was in this case from 1763.

Margaret Rowe, who went by the name Ann, was born in Suffolk in 1742, the daughter of local farmer John Rowe. On 3rd July 1759, the young maid entered into a good marriage with John Beddingfield, another local farmer. He was the 24-year-old son of a well-to-do family in Sternfield. Everyone agreed that Ann had married well and, with the help of his parents, John set the couple up in a well-positioned and productive farm close to the village.

By all accounts, Ann seemed content in the early years of her marriage, bearing two children and settling in well as the wife of a wealthy country farmer. She had status, money and her own domestic staff. But all this was about to change with the appearance of a new young farm worker onto the estate.

Nineteen-year-old Richard Ringe arrived at the couple's farm in 1761. His living quarters were in the Beddingfield house and within a few months he and Ann had become lovers. As their devotion to each other developed, it was Ann who first muted the idea of despatching John Beddingfield and living together on the proceeds from the dead man's estate. In his later confession, Ringe claimed he was a reluctant volunteer to the ill-fated scheme.

The couple's murder plans were unsophisticated and naïve. On one occasion Ringe asked an unwilling maidservant to add some poison he had purchased to the rum and milk her master consumed each morning. He then tried to add arsenic to John's drinking water, the latter noticing a white deposit in the water basin before steadfastly refusing to drink.

Ann was equally reckless in her approach. On one occasion she confided in one of the maids, saying, 'Help me to put on my ear-rings; but I shall not wear them much longer, for I shall have new black ones. It will not be long before somebody in the house dies, and I believe it will be your master.'

Alert to any opportunity, the hapless couple decided to take their chances on the night of 27th July 1762. John returned from an evening of drinking with a neighbouring farmer to find his marriage bed empty. Finding Ann sharing the room next door with one of the maidservants, John asked her to return to his bed. She refused and an argument ensued.

The attack on the unsuspecting Beddingfield was as ill-thought out as all of the previous attempts at murder. Ringe entered the farmer's bedroom in the early hours to strangle him with a piece of cord. Beddingfield awoke from his slumber to fend off the attack and in the struggle both men fell off the bed. Before Ringe had finally finished him off, most of the household had been roused by the noise of the fight.

Ringe's post-murder tactics continued to beggar belief. He immediately staggered through into the next room, announcing to Ann and a stunned maidservant that, 'I have done for him.' Ann simply replied, 'Then I am easy', before instructing the domestic servant to hold her tongue and keep quiet about the incident.

Aroused from their slumber, the domestic staff entered Beddingfield's room to find him dead, his shirt collar ripped and his neck bruised and swollen. A message was sent to the farmer's parents who asked for a surgeon to be called. Ann made it clear that this was unnecessary as her husband was already dead.

In the initial aftermath of the killing it seemed as if the young lovers might actually get away with the crime. The coroner's inquest the following day took only a short time to reach the wholly inaccurate verdict that John Beddingfield had died of natural causes, summed up as 'death by falling out of bed'. None of the domestic servants was called to give evidence.

However, their luck was short-lived. Waiting until she had received her wages for the previous quarter, one of the maidservants first told her parents and then went to the local constable with the full story. The police then issued a warrant for the arrest of the two lovers.

Ringe made no attempt to escape the long arm of the law, knowing that his days were numbered. He stayed in the Beddingfield house and was arrested the next day and taken to Ipswich gaol. Ann fled but was apprehended two days later.

During their trial at the Ipswich Lent Assizes in March 1763, Ringe confessed to the crime, leaving Ann to plead her innocence, supported by the police surgeon who continued, steadfastly, to believe that the death was due to natural causes. But at the outcome of the trial, the jury found both guilty as charged. Ann later confessed in Ipswich prison a week before her death.

The lovers were both executed on 8th April 1763 on the heath of Rushmere St Andrew, near Ipswich. In a speech to the crowd, Ringe warned other young men against the dangers of being influenced by wicked women and extolled the virtue of chastity. He was hanged for his part in the murder of John Beddingfield.

For her part, Ann was condemned to be burnt at the stake for husband murder, or petty treason. In the event, she shared the platform with her lover and at the appointed time, in front of the large assembled crowd, was strangled by her executioner before being burnt. Ringe's body was dissected after death in accordance with the Murder Act of 1752.

It seems that this shocking crime, which ultimately resulted in the deaths of three people, came about largely as a result of one young woman whose romantic notions clouded her very sense of reason and rationality.

SUFFOLK'S MYSTERIOUS STONES

❁

Legends about standing stones and the strange powers they embody are commonplace in most parts of Britain. And, while Suffolk may have comparatively fewer mysterious stones than other counties, the stories surrounding those that do exist are no less appealing, fascinating and mystifying.

Many of the county's more unusual stones have served as direction or boundary markers. Other static and seemingly immovable boulders were sited at common meeting points. And while some are naturally occurring rocks, or 'erratics', brought down by the movement of glaciers during the last Ice Age, a fair number have been moved and positioned by earlier generations for ritualistic or functional purposes or to mark key events in history.

Examples of direction and boundary markers include the 'Stockton Stone', just north of Beccles and on the border between Norfolk and Suffolk. This sandstone erratic lies on a grassy patch of land along the A146 and is thought to be a track marker. It is also infamous as being one of the few East Anglian stones with a curse. Legend has it that anyone who moves the stone will die within a year. True or not, the stone was moved during the straightening of the road in the 1930s and one of the workers involved did die suddenly.

The illusive 'Groaning Stone' at Debenham in mid Suffolk is also believed to be a direction marker, situated as it is along a track heading west from the north end of the village.

Standing stone at Stockton near Beccles.

Locals claim the stone moves and groans at midnight, with the striking of the church clock.

At Bungay, in the north-east of the county, can be found the 'Druid's Stone' an embedded granite erratic which stands in the churchyard of St Mary's. Many have claimed that this marks the spot of earlier Pagan rituals and stories abound about the running and dancing games that can be performed around the boulder to summon the Devil. It is more likely to be a direction stone, extracted from the ruins of nearby Bungay Castle.

In contrast, the 'Chediston Stone' near Halesworth is claimed by some to have been a direction marker for smugglers bringing contraband in from the coast some ten miles away. The stone is thought to have been much taller in the past (as much as 30 feet in height), reduced to its present

The Druid's stone in St Mary's churchyard, Bungay.

stature of around six feet as a result of its being broken up by locals and used to make walls. The sandstone boulder, which stands in a garden at the edge of the village, is believed to derive its name from the Old English 'Ceddes Stan', or 'Cedd's Stone' which gave the village its name. Some historians have speculated that it must therefore have had connections to St Cedd who preached nearby, although this is by no means certain.

Close to the village of Wattisham, south of Stowmarket, lies another sandstone direction marker. At less than three feet tall, the 'Wattisham Stone' sits at the junction of three roads. Like its counterpart in Debenham, the stone is believed to move at the sound of chiming, in this case from the bells of the church tower in nearby Bildeston.

Mysterious stones which mark common meeting points from the past are also much in evidence. The 'Hiring Stone' at Fornham St Martin, near Bury St Edmunds, is a good example. Standing in the yard of a working farm, the small stone occupies a spot where agricultural labourers are said to have been paid and hired.

In comparison, the jagged 'Preaching Stone' in the town of Mendlesham is held to have been a common rallying point for medieval friars to deliver their sermons, while the erratic 'Druid Stone' in the village of Wenhaston is thought to have been a place of Pagan worship.

Other stones have equally intriguing stories. The 'Devil's Stone' in the nearby village of Middleton is said to have been a meeting point for local witches and a place where Satan's voice could be summoned. Similarly, the 'Witches' Stones' in Lowestoft, a collection of small, roughly cemented, rocks near to Cart Score, are alleged to have been a regular haunt of Amy Duny, one of two Lowestoft women tried and hanged for witchcraft in 1665 (see chapter 4). The stones themselves are believed to be weather makers, bringing rain if doused in water.

Not far away, in the churchyard of St Michael's in the village of Oulton, is 'George Edward's Stone'. This granite rock, which stands at over four feet in height, was hauled up from the bed of nearby Lake Lothing when the modern harbour of Lowestoft was created in the 19th century. Engraved with George Edward's epitaph, the standing stone is rumoured to be the meeting place of fairies at key times throughout the year.

At least two stones are alleged to have been sacrificial sites. The first one is the 'Baal Stone' at Whepstead near Bury St Edmunds and the other is 'Wulf's Stone', in the village of Woolverstone, south of Ipswich. The latter is said to be the point at which the Viking King Wulf sacrificed a local woman while raiding the area sometime before the tenth century.

The other common category of unusual stones is those that mark key events in history. This includes the

An early Christian stone cross in St Botolph's church, Iken.

'Highwayman's Stone' in Barrow, to the east of Newmarket, believed to be the spot on which a local villain was hanged in 1789 for attempting to shoot a resident of Barrow Hall who was collecting parish tithes. The stone apparently turns at midnight every new year's eve. Further south, can be found the 'Hartest Stone', a large limestone rock which sits on the village green. It is said to have been sited by local men to mark battle victories in the War of the Spanish Succession and it too is supposed to turn round when the clock strikes midnight. Anybody planning on staying up to watch this phenomenon is then told that it will only happen when the stone can actually hear the chimes for itself!

Alongside the naturally occurring rocks and sited boulders, there are also a number of carefully crafted stone icons throughout Suffolk. Good examples can be found in the churchyards of Wortham, Woolpit and Kedington, although the best early Christian stone cross can be found inside the church of St Botolph in Iken on the Alde Estuary. It is decorated with Anglo-Saxon interlace patterns and a mythical beast, and is thought to have been three metres high originally. The cross was found during excavations of the church in 1977, built into the base of the church tower. It is thought to date from the ninth or tenth century, the church itself looking down over the earlier site of an Anglo-Saxon cemetery. Local historians believe that it may have been a memorial to St Botolph when his body was moved from the site.

Finally, there are the stones which defy explanation or understanding. Most notably, these include the 'Blaxhall Stone', north of Woodbridge. This round sandstone erratic stands in the yard of a farm and is alleged to grow in size year by year. Over 150,000 years old, the stone currently weighs about five tons. To this we could add other magical stones which are said to be located in various towns and villages but which appear to have disappeared from the public gaze.

Suffolk may not have a huge volume of mysterious stones across its rural landscape, but those that do exist are worth recognising and celebrating for the richness and diversity of the tales that surround them.

A WARTIME MURDER

───────────❁───────────

Claude Fiske was the first to see the body, at around eight o'clock on the morning of Thursday, 9th November 1944, as he cycled along Ellough Road and past Green Lane towards Beccles. The electrician's mate did not need to linger long before realising that the young woman lying face down in the ditch was indeed dead. Arriving hurriedly at his workplace he telephoned the town's police station and raised the curtain on one of the most brutal and largely unknown dramas in wartime Suffolk – the murder of Winnie Evans.

Detective Inspector Read of the East Suffolk force took charge of the investigation, travelling to the scene with a team of CID officers. He readily determined that the young woman's death had been no accident – the visible injuries on her body suggesting that she had been seriously assaulted and suffocated in the mud at the bottom of the ditch. The detectives also found a button from a military greatcoat lying near the body and were instructed by Read to begin the task of visiting all of the nearby airbases to see if anyone knew anything about the events that had led to the woman's death.

DI Read recognised that the nature of the crime and the enormity of the task at hand would require more expertise and manpower than he could provide during a period of war. The area around Beccles contained a number of heavily populated British and American air bases and a camp of Italian prisoners of war. To ensure that the crime was investigated efficiently and effectively, Read took the decision to call Scotland Yard and was joined later that day by Detective Chief Inspector Ted Greeno, Detective Sergeant Hodge and Doctor Keith Simpson, a Home Office pathologist. Having been briefed by Read, the experienced and capable DCI Greeno wasted no time in taking over the investigation. Doctor Simpson requested that the body be taken to Beccles hospital for a post-mortem examination.

The detectives' swift response led to some immediate results. The victim was identified as Winifred Mary Evans, a 27-year-old Women's Auxiliary Air Force (WAAF) officer, who was working as a wireless operator on the nearby RAF airfield at Ellough. One of her friends, Corporal Margaret Johns, was able to tell the detectives much of what had occurred that Wednesday evening prior to Winnie's untimely death. This included her description of an encounter with Arthur Heys, an airman from Colne in Lancashire, who was to become the detectives' primary suspect in the weeks and months that followed.

Piecing together the events of Wednesday, 8th November 1944, the detectives learnt that Winnie had gone with friends to an evening dance at a nearby American air base. While popular with her friends, the hapless wireless operator was described as quiet and 'rather reserved'. Unlike some of her colleagues, she was not given to casual romances.

Due back at the Ellough airfield for an 11.30 pm shift, Winnie had left the dance with Corporal Johns – both women walking back to their billet. Winnie had then changed quickly before setting out to walk the additional mile to base headquarters on a chilly November night. She declined Corporal Johns' invitation to accompany her.

Sometime shortly after setting out from the billet, Winnie was murdered in a ditch along the Ellough Road – the post-mortem results confirming that she had suffocated in the mud while being raped.

The interview with Corporal Johns produced one additional, and crucial, revelation. After saying goodbye to her friend, Johns had visited the women's ablutions hut. As she entered the building and switched on the light, she was startled to see a man in an RAF uniform, swaying unsteadily. Pulling rank and concerned by the man's obvious drunkenness, Johns challenged him and asked him to explain what he was doing. He claimed to be lost and as Johns helped him out of the building the airman made a clumsy pass at her. She pushed him off and watched him head off down the road – the same route that Winnie had taken only a short time before.

It fell to local detectives to follow up the lead presented by Corporal Johns. The mystery airman had said he was based at the No. 1 camp site, so the officers asked Johns to accompany them to an afternoon parade at the camp, where she easily picked out the man she had spoken to that fateful night. The 37-year-old Arthur Heys was taken to Beccles police station for questioning by the Scotland Yard detectives.

DCI Greeno could hardly believe his luck. Facing Heys, he noticed that one of the airman's jigger buttons was missing. Interviews with other personnel at the camp also revealed that Heys had been out socialising that Wednesday evening at a dance in Beccles. He had been drinking heavily and had not returned to his billet until the early hours of Thursday morning. The next day he had been seen rising early to clean his shoes and uniform.

During questioning, Greeno learnt that Heys was married with a young family and had just returned from a period of leave some days before. Heys confirmed that he had been out drinking and dancing on the night of the murder. He said his enjoyment had been marred at the end of the evening when he discovered that his bicycle had been stolen and he had been forced to walk back to his camp. In his statement, he first claimed that he had returned directly to the camp, arriving at around 12.30 am. Under further questioning, he admitted to Greeno that he had gone to the WAAF camp and had spoken to Corporal Johns, but still claimed to have arrived back at his own billet by 12.30 am and denied rising early to clean his shoes or uniform. He steadfastly refused to admit to any wrongdoing and having submitted a sample of hair for forensic comparison was returned to his camp.

While much of the evidence was circumstantial, Greeno continued to build a strong case against Heys. A search of the airman's belongings produced the clothes he had been wearing on the night of the dance. Forensic examination identified some blood stains on his tunic and brick dust on his shoes which matched samples taken from both Winnie's body and the ditch. Hairs found on the victim's clothes also appeared to be similar to those taken from Heys during the interrogation.

Given the weight of evidence against Heys, the Director of Public Prosecutions allowed the prosecution to go ahead and following further questioning on 5th December 1944, Heys was charged with the murder and spent the Christmas and New Year period in Norwich prison awaiting trial and visited only by his wife who made the long journey down from Lancashire.

Winifred Mary Evans was finally laid to rest in a sombre and sparsely attended funeral at All Saints' church, close to her family home in Harlesden, West London, on 16th December. The burial, like the crime itself, attracted surprisingly little attention in the press, given the events being played out on the global stage.

The committal proceedings against Arthur Heys began in the Beccles courtroom on 10th January 1945. After outlining the course of events and the case against him, the prosecution called 23 witnesses to give evidence on the first day alone. Alongside the testimony from Corporal Johns, airman Victor Redmonds told the court that Heys had returned to his bed between 1.00 am and 1.30 am on the Thursday morning. He also said that he had observed how dirty Heys' shoes had been and had noticed scratches on the hands of the accused.

As the committal continued, there was to be a dramatic turn of events. At the end of the second day's hearing, when Greeno returned to Beccles police station, he was passed a letter that had been received by Hey's Commanding Officer. It read:

'Will you please give this letter to the solicitors for the airman who is so wrongfully accused of murdering Winnie Evans? I want to state I am responsible for the above-mentioned girl's death. I had arranged to meet her at the bottom of the road where the body was found, at midnight. When I arrived she was not there. I waited some time, and decided to walk down towards the WAAF quarters. Just before I reached this I heard a voice and stood close to the hedge. I heard footsteps. It proved to be an airman. I don't think he saw me. I then saw someone I recognised was Winnie. She said I should not have come down to meet her. A WAAF friend had offered to go along with her, as the airman ahead was drunk and had lost his way. She had her bicycle with her; no one will ever find this …'.

Greeno was unconvinced by the letter. In fact, he was now even more certain that they had got their man and the letter had been penned by Heys himself. Who else could have known that the airman was lost apart from Heys and Corporal Johns? Winnie had left Johns before Heys arrived, so could not possibly have known. The mystery was how Heys had managed to post the letter while on remand in Norwich. Greeno's subsequent investigations revealed that the blue pencil used to write the note was similar to those made available to prisoners in the gaol. He concluded that Heys must have arranged for the note to be smuggled out and posted.

Handwriting samples were taken and both they and the letter were subjected to cross-examination by the head of Scotland Yard's Fingerprint Bureau. The latter was in no doubt that the handwriting samples were produced by the same man who had written the alleged confession.

Arthur Heys' trial began in Bury St Edmunds on Monday, 22nd January 1945 and lasted for three days. While the evidence against him remained largely circumstantial, it was weighty. The main plank of the airman's defence was the so-called confession letter, which his defence claimed had been written by the real killer.

The witnesses repeated the same evidence that had been presented at the earlier committal proceedings. But Greeno was to present additional information that was to seal Heys' fate. He described the conclusions of the handwriting examination and outlined how Heys could have smuggled the letter out of Norwich prison. Despite a robust challenge from the defence team and a confident performance by Heys when questioned, the evidence added greatly to the already strong case against the airman.

The jury took only 40 minutes to reach its verdict of 'guilty'. Asked if he knew of any reason why the sentence of death should not be passed on him, Heys replied assertively, 'God knows I am innocent of this foul crime. I know God will look after me. I am not afraid.'

With all of his appeals rejected, Heys faced the death penalty for his crime and was duly hanged on Tuesday, 13th March 1945. In the midst of a global conflict which would leave millions dead and millions more wounded and displaced, this was a largely overlooked and unreported crime of sexual violence and a tragic and untimely end for a quiet young woman whose only concern that cold November night had been to serve her country in the smoky wireless room of a small Suffolk airbase.

BIBLIOGRAPHY

———————— ❀ ————————

A variety of source materials were used in the research for this book, including a wealth of local newspapers and journals – a list far too long to include here. However, the following books may be of interest to those wishing to read more about some of the murder and mystery stories featured in this compilation:

Bibliography
Church, R, *Murder in East Anglia*, Robert Hale, 1987
Gatrell, V, *The Hanging Tree: Execution and the English People 1770-1868*, Oxford University Press, 1994
Glyde, J, *Folklore and Customs of Suffolk*, EP Publishing Limited, 1976
Greengrass, H, and Scott-Davies, A, *Ghosts of Bury St Edmunds*, Artscape, 2000
Haining, P, *The Supernatural Coast: Unexplained Mysteries of East Anglia*, Robert Hale, 1992
Haining, P, Where *the Eagle Landed: The Mystery of the German Invasion of Britain*, 1940, Robson, 2004
Hole, C, *Witchcraft in England*, Fitzhouse, 1990
Maple, Eric, *Supernatural England*, Robert Hale, 1977
Pennick, N, *Secrets of East Anglian Magic*, Robert Hale, 1995
Puttick, B, *Ghosts of Suffolk*, Countryside Books, 1998

ACKNOWLEDGEMENTS

---❀---

This book could not have been written without the kind help and invaluable assistance of my immediate family and close friends and a host of local characters who were eager to provide me with information and insights of which I would otherwise have been unaware.

My thanks must go firstly to my publishers, who have provided me with this opportunity to set down a series of tales from a county for which I have so much affection. The Suffolk Public Record Office provided me with much of the excellent source material for the crime stories featured in the book. Equally important were the online archives of the Foxearth and District Local History Society – an exceptional resource for any local writer or historian.

I am also particularly indebted to the following for their contributions: Tony Morley; Colin and Frankie Denny; Georgina and Adrian King; my parents Arnold and Christine Mower; and Kevin Garrod. Most importantly, I must thank my wife Jacqueline who has, alongside a cat called Monty, provided me with constant inspiration throughout many months of writing and research. She also worked tirelessly in producing maps, reviewing early drafts and taking photographs of haunted buildings, moss-covered boulders and eerie graveyards. She gets to visit all the best places.